Microsoft® Windows Vista

PEARSON
Prentice Hall

Harlow, England • London • New York • Boston • San Francisco • Toronto • Sydney • Singapore • Hong Kong
Tokyo • Seoul • Taipei • New Delhi • Cape Town • Madrid • Mexico City • Amsterdam • Munich • Paris • Milan

PEARSON EDUCATION LIMITED

Edinburgh Gate
Harlow CM20 2JE
Tel: +44 (0)1279 623623
Fax: +44 (0)1279 431059
Website: www.pearsoned.co.uk

First published in Great Britain in 2009

ISBN: 978–0–273–72349–3

British Library Cataloguing-in-Publication Data
A catalogue record for this book is available from the British Library

Library of Congress Cataloging-in-Publication Data
Ballew, Joli.
   Microsoft Windows Vista in simple steps / Joli Ballew. -- 1st ed.
      p. cm.
   ISBN 978-0-273-72349-3 (pbk.)
   1. Microsoft Windows (Computer file) 2. Operating systems (Computers) I. Title.
   QA76.76.O63B3594 2009
   005.4'46--dc22
                          2009009531

10 9 8 7 6 5 4 3 2 1
13 12 11 10 09

Designed by pentacorbig, High Wycombe
Typeset in 11/14 pt ITC Stone Sans by 3
Printed and bound in Great Britain by Ashford Colour Press Ltd, Gosport, Hants

The publisher's policy is to use paper manufactured from sustainable forests.

Microsoft®

Windows Vista

in Simple steps

Joli Ballew

Use your computer with confidence

Get to grips with practical computing tasks with minimal time, fuss and bother.

In Simple Steps guides guarantee immediate results. They tell you everything you need to know on a specific application; from the most essential tasks to master, to every activity you'll want to accomplish, through to solving the most common problems you'll encounter.

Helpful features

To build your confidence and help you to get the most out of your computer, practical hints, tips and shortcuts feature on every page:

 ALERT: Explains and provides practical solutions to the most commonly encountered problems

 HOT TIP: Time and effort saving shortcuts

 SEE ALSO: Points you to other related tasks and information

 DID YOU KNOW? Additional features to explore

WHAT DOES THIS MEAN?
Jargon and technical terms explained in plain English

Practical. Simple. Fast.

Dedication:

For Mom and Papa John, may you both rest in peace.

Author acknowledgments:

I just love writing for Pearson Education, and these *In Simple Steps* books prove it. Three books in almost as many months! It's wonderful working with Steve Temblett, Laura Blake and the rest of the gang. It's not often I find a team that works so well together.

I'd also like to acknowledge my agent, Neil Salkind, who works hard for me always, and my family, Dad, Jennifer, and Cosmo. I wish my mom could be here to see these books; she would have enjoyed them. You may see her in a few of the pictures here.

Contents at a glance

Top 10 Vista Problems Solved

Contents

2 Computing essentials

3 Perform tasks with Windows Vista

4 Files and folders

5 Connecting to and surfing the Internet

6 Working with email

7 Stay secure

8 Install hardware

9 Windows Media Player

Top 10 Vista Tips

Tip 1: Change the desktop background and screen saver

1 Right-click an empty area of the desktop.

2 Click Personalize.

3 Click Desktop Background.

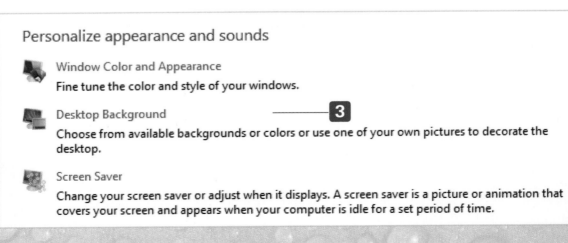

4 For Location, select Windows Wallpapers. If it is not chosen already, click the down arrow to locate it.

5 Use the scroll bars to locate the wallpaper to use as your desktop background.

6 Select a background to use.

7 Select a positioning option (the default is the most common).

8 Click OK.

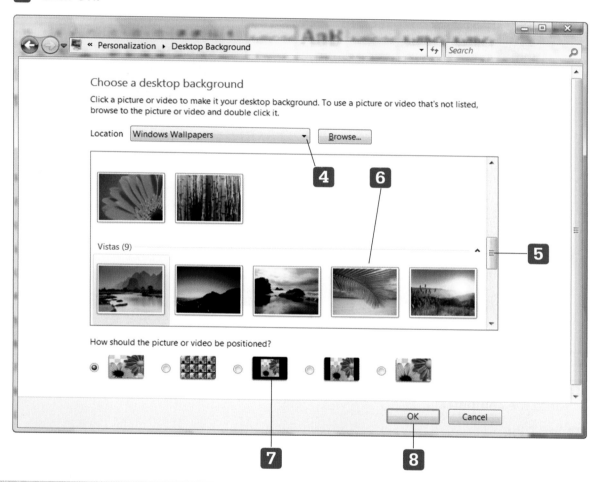

9 Click Screen Saver.

Screen Saver

Change your screen saver or adjust when it displays. A screen saver is a picture or animation that covers your screen and appears when your computer is idle for a set period of time.

10 Click the arrow to see the available screen saver and select one.

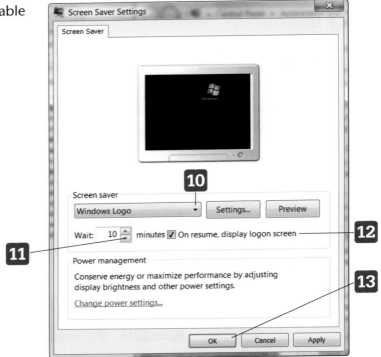

11 Use the arrows to change how long to wait before the screen saver is enabled.

12 If desired, click On resume, display logon screen to require a password to log back into the computer.

13 Click OK.

14 Click the X in the Personalization window to close it.

Tip 2: Locate and start a program

1 Click Start.

2 Click All Programs.

3 If necessary, use the scroll bars to locate the program to open.

4 Click the name of the program to open it.

5 Click the X in the top right corner to close the application.

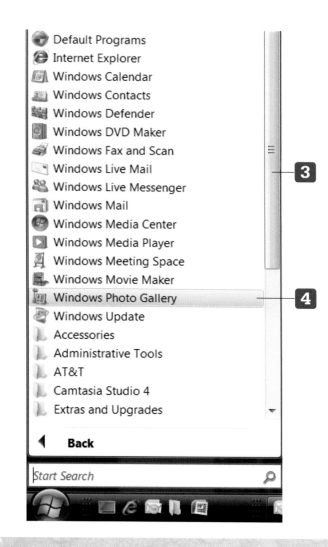

Tip 3: Send an email

1 Open Windows Mail and click Create Mail.

2 Type the recipient's email address in the To line. If you want to add additional names, separate each email address by a semicolon.

3 Type a subject in the Subject field.

4 Type the message in the body pane.

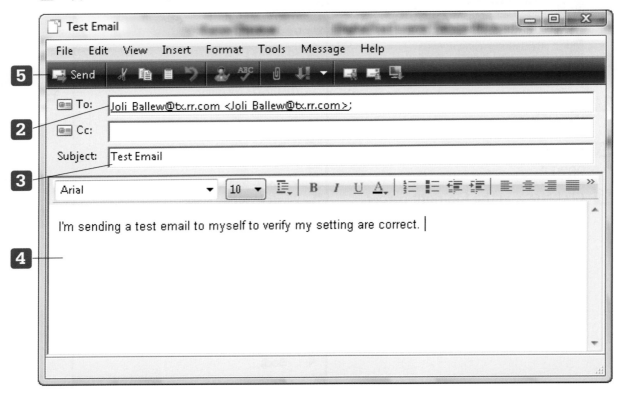

5 Click Send.

 HOT TIP: If you get an error that something is wrong with your settings, click Tools, click Accounts, select your email account, and click Properties. You can then retype your account information, password, or other property.

Tip 4: Find information on the Internet

1 Open Internet Explorer. A website will probably open automatically.

2 To open a new website, drag your mouse across the website name to select it. Do not drag your mouse over the http://www part of the address.

3 Type the name of the website you'd like to visit in the address bar. Try amazon.com.

4 Press Enter on the keyboard.

 HOT TIP: You can usually locate a company's website by typing its name in between http://www and .com. For instance, http://www.microsoft.com, or locate a site based on content such as http://www.weather.com.

Tip 5: Upload pictures from a digital camera

1 Connect the device. If applicable, turn it on.

2 When prompted, choose Import Pictures using Windows.

3 Type a descriptive name for the group of pictures you're importing.

4 Click Import.

 HOT TIP: During the import process you'll see an option to delete the images from the camera or the memory card after the pictures have been imported. Select this as you desire.

Tip 6: Watch a DVD

1 Find the button on the PC's tower, keyboard or laptop that opens the DVD drive door. Press it.

2 Place the DVD in the door and press the button again to close it.

3 When prompted, choose Play DVD movie using Windows Media Player.

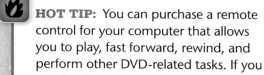

HOT TIP: You can purchase a remote control for your computer that allows you to play, fast forward, rewind, and perform other DVD-related tasks. If you watch a lot of DVDs on your computer, it might be a good purchase.

Tip 7: Listen to a music CD

1 Find the button on the PC's tower, keyboard or laptop that opens the CD drive door. Press it.

2 Place the CD in the door and press the button again to close it.

3 When prompted, choose Play CD movie using Windows Media Player.

Tip 8: Back up data to a USB drive

1 Click Start and click Computer.

2 Locate the USB drive. (Leave this window open.)

3 Locate a folder to copy.

4 Position the windows so you can see them both.

5 Right-click the folder to copy.

6 While holding down the right mouse key, drag the folder to the new location.

7 Drop it there.

8 Choose Copy Here.

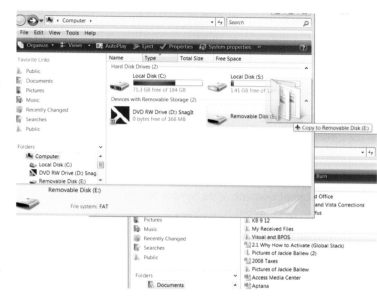

Tip 9: Write a letter

1 Click Start.

2 In the Start Search window, type Notepad.

3 Click Notepad under Programs. (Note that you may see other results, as shown here.)

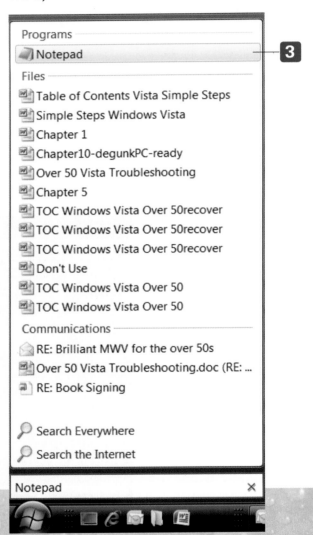

4 Click once inside Notepad and start typing.

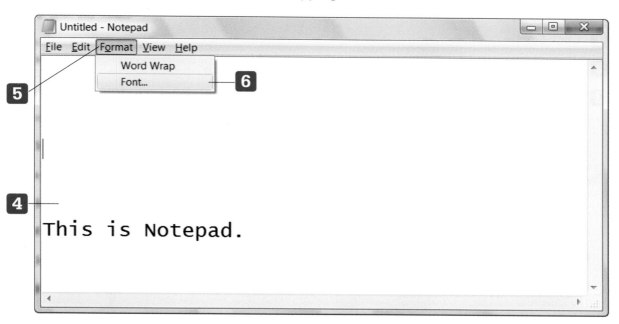

5 To change the font or font size, select the typed text and click Format.

6 Click Font.

7 Use the scroll bars to locate a font. Select the font you like.

8 Select a font style.

9 Select a font size.

10 Click OK.

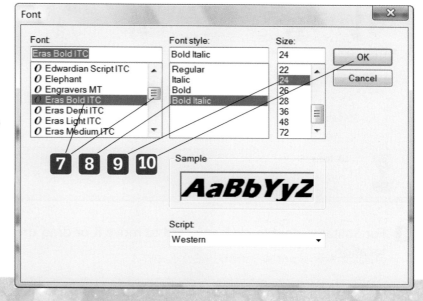

HOT TIP: A preview of the font will appear in the Font dialogue box.

Tip 10: Play a game

1 Click Start.

2 Click Games.

3 Double-click any game to begin.

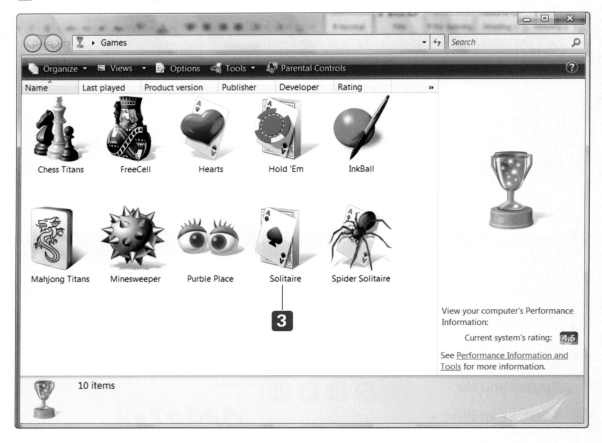

4 For Solitaire, double-click any card to move it or drag the card to the desired location.

1 Getting started with Windows Vista

Introduction

Congratulations on your new Windows Vista PC; you're in for a treat and a few surprises too! Windows Vista has a ton of great features, runs faster and is easier to use than previous Microsoft operating systems. With Vista, you can create text documents, upload and edit photos from your digital camera, make movies from your personal video footage, manage and listen to music, surf the Internet, send and receive email, get up-to-the-minute weather and news, and more, all without purchasing anything else.

You don't need to be a computer guru to use Windows Vista; in fact, you don't have to know anything at all. Its interface is intuitive. The Start button offers a place to access just about everything you'll need, from photos to music to email; the Recycle Bin holds stuff you've deleted; and the Sidebar offers a bar full of *gadgets* you are likely to want to access, like a clock, the weather and news headlines. In this first chapter you will discover how little you need to know (and learn) to get started with Windows Vista.

Important: Windows Vista comes in several editions and computer manufacturers often add their own touches. As a result, your screen may not look exactly like what you'll see in the screenshots in this book (but it'll be close).

Start Windows Vista

Windows Vista is the most important software installed on your computer. Although you probably have other software programs (like Microsoft Office or Photoshop Elements), Windows Vista is your computer's *operating system* and thus it's what allows *you* to *operate* your computer's *system*. You will use Windows Vista to find things you have stored on your computer, connect to the Internet, enable you to move the mouse and see the pointer move on the screen, and print, among other things. The operating system is what allows you to communicate with your PC. Before you can use Windows Vista, you have to start it.

1 If applicable, open the laptop's lid.

2 Press the Start button to turn on the computer.

3 If applicable, press the Start button on the computer monitor.

? DID YOU KNOW?
Starting a computer is also called 'booting' it.

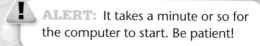

! ALERT: It takes a minute or so for the computer to start. Be patient!

Activate Windows Vista

If you are starting Vista for the first time and you're on a new PC (or laptop), you'll be prompted to enter some information. Specifically, you'll type your name as you'd like it to appear on your Start menu (capital letters count), activate Windows Vista and, if desired, register your copy of Windows Vista. It's important to know that while activation is mandatory, registration is not.

1 Follow the directions on the screen, clicking Next to move from one page of the activation wizard to the next.

2 When prompted to register, remember, registration is optional. You can skip this part.

3 When you have activated Vista, wait a few seconds for Windows Vista to initialise.

4 Click the Start button at the bottom of the Windows Vista screen to view your user name.

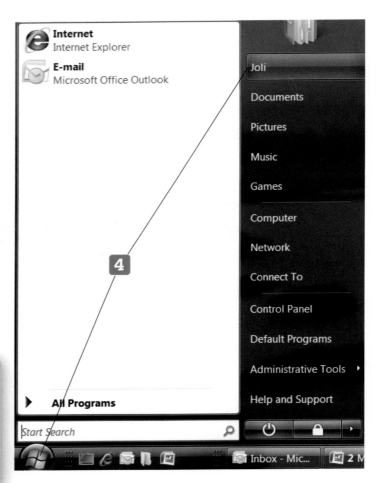

? DID YOU KNOW?

Activation is mandatory, and if you do not activate Windows within the 30-day time frame, Windows Vista will lose all functionality – except for the activation process.

! ALERT: To activate and register Windows Vista during the initial set-up, you'll have to be connected to the Internet. Alternatively, you can use the phone number provided to activate over the phone.

? DID YOU KNOW?

When you register you offer personal identification about yourself, including your email address.

View computer details

When you first start Windows Vista, the Welcome Center opens. There are at least two sections: Get started with Windows and Offers from Microsoft, and perhaps others not included here. Often computer manufacturers add their own listings and links to help you learn about your computer and the applications they've installed on it, as well as links to their own Help files or website. From the Welcome Center you can view details about your computer, among other things.

1 With the Welcome Center open, click View computer details.

2 Read the details regarding your computer.

3 If you do not want the Welcome Center to open every time you start Windows Vista, remove the tick mark from Run at startup.

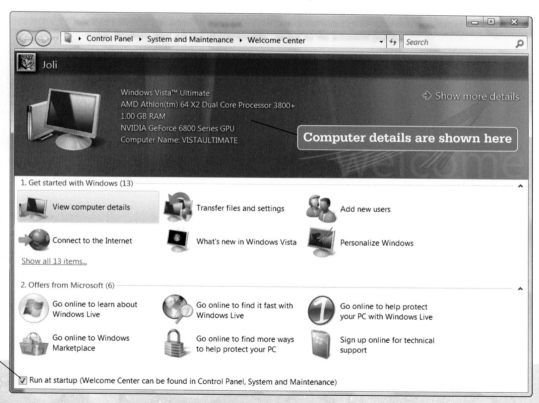

Computer details are shown here

? DID YOU KNOW?

The Welcome Center can be found by typing Welcome in the Start search window.

Empty the Recycle Bin

The Recycle Bin holds deleted files until you decide to empty it. The Recycle Bin serves as a safeguard, allowing you to recover items accidentally deleted, or items you thought you no longer wanted but later decide you need.

1 Locate the Recycle Bin on the desktop and point to it with the mouse.

2 Right-click the Recycle Bin.

3 Choose Empty Recycle Bin.

4 Click Yes.

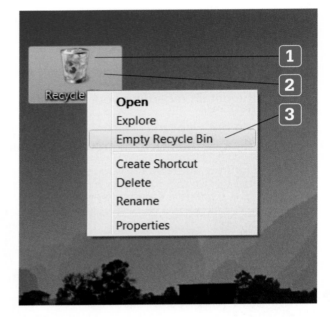

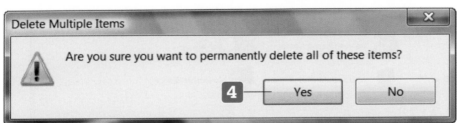

ALERT: Once you empty the Recycle Bin, the items in it are gone for ever.

HOT TIP: You can close the Recycle Bin by clicking the X in the top right corner.

Restore data using the Recycle Bin

If you delete something that you decide you later want to keep or need, you can 'restore' it from the Recycle Bin. That is, unless you've emptied the Recycle Bin since deleting the item!

1. Double-click the Recycle Bin.

2. Right-click the file to recover.

3. Click Restore.

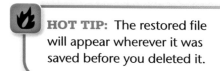

HOT TIP: The restored file will appear wherever it was saved before you deleted it.

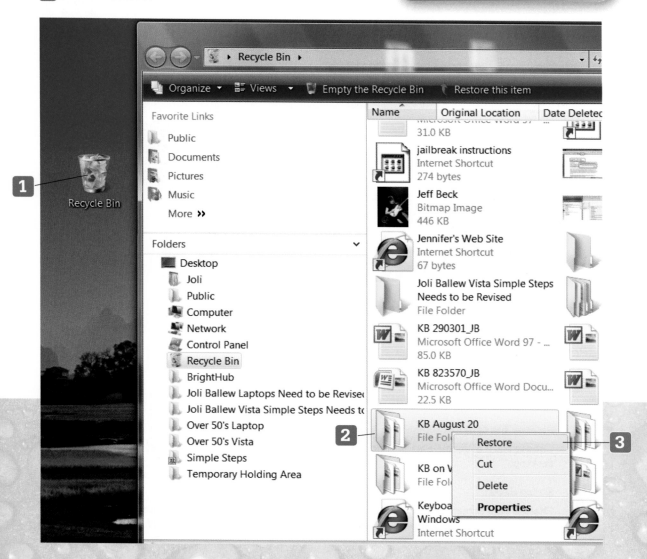

Change the desktop background

One of the first things you may like to do when you get a new PC or upgrade an older one is to personalise the picture on the desktop. That picture is called the background.

1 Right-click an empty area of the desktop.

2 Click Personalize.

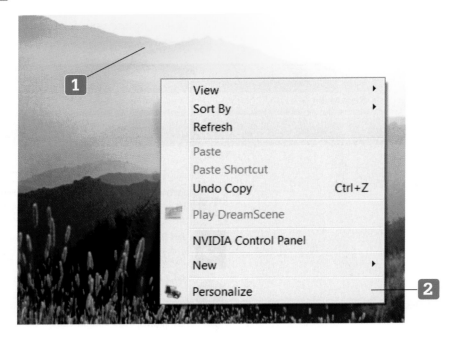

3 Click Desktop Background.

Personalize appearance and sounds

Window Color and Appearance
Fine tune the color and style of your windows.

Desktop Background ──────────── **3**
Choose from available backgrounds or colors or use one of your own pictures to decorate the desktop.

Screen Saver
Change your screen saver or adjust when it displays. A screen saver is a picture or animation that covers your screen and appears when your computer is idle for a set period of time.

4. For Location, select Windows Wallpapers. If it is not chosen already, click the down arrow to locate it.

5. Use the scroll bars to locate the wallpaper to use as your desktop background.

6. Select a background to use.

7. Select a positioning option (the default is the most common).

8. Click OK.

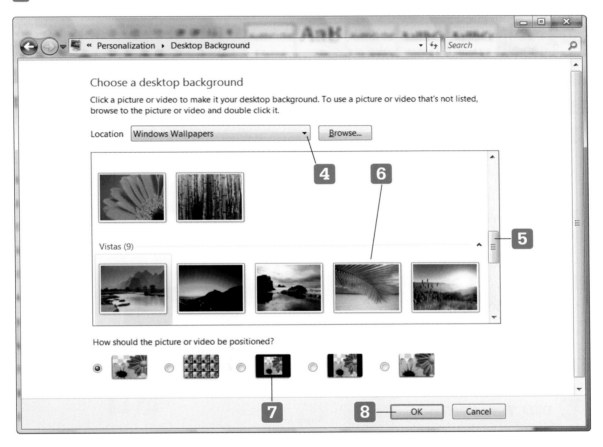

DID YOU KNOW?

You can click the Browse button to locate a picture you've taken, acquired or otherwise saved to your computer and use it for a desktop background. Pictures are usually found in the Pictures folder.

Change the screen saver

A screen saver is a picture or animation that covers your screen and appears after your computer has been idle for a specific amount of time that you set. Screen savers are used either for visual enhancement or as a security feature. For security, you can configure your screen saver to require a password on waking up, which happens when you move the mouse or hit a key on the keyboard. Requiring a password means that once the screen saver is running, no one can log onto your computer but you, by typing in your password when prompted.

1 Right-click an empty area of the desktop.

2 Click Personalize.

3 Click Screen Saver.

4 Click the arrow to see the available screen saver and select one.

 Screen Saver

Change your screen saver or adjust when it displays. A screen saver is a picture or animation that covers your screen and appears when your computer is idle for a set period of time.

5 Use the arrows to change how long to wait before the screen saver is enabled.

6 If desired, click On resume, display logon screen to require a password to log back into the computer.

7 Click OK.

? DID YOU KNOW?
It used to be that screen savers 'saved' your computer screen from image burn-in, but that is no longer the case.

? DID YOU KNOW?
Select Photos and your screen saver will be a slide show of photos stored in your Pictures folder.

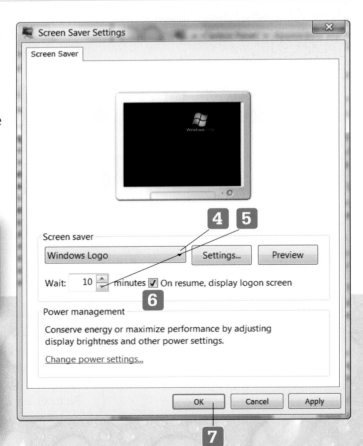

Add desktop icons

When Windows Vista started the first time, it may have had only one item on the desktop, the Recycle Bin. Alternatively, it may have had 20 or more. What appears on your desktop the first time Windows boots up depends on a number of factors, including who manufactured and/or installed the PC.

1 Right-click an empty area of the desktop.

2 Click Personalize.

3 Click Change desktop icons.

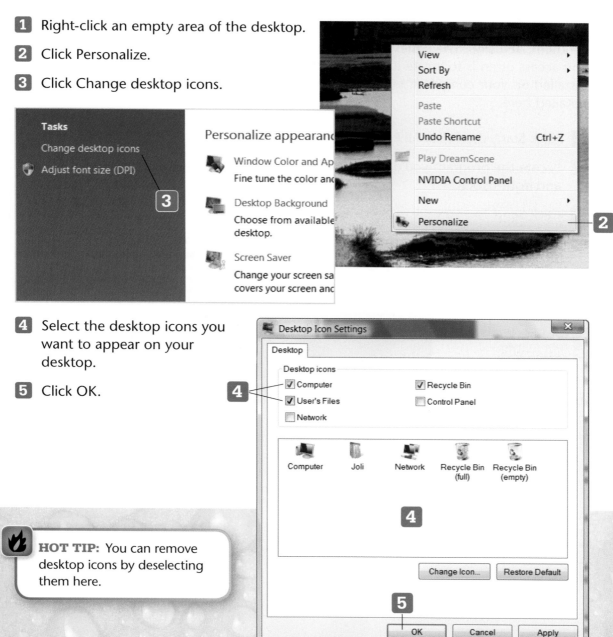

4 Select the desktop icons you want to appear on your desktop.

5 Click OK.

HOT TIP: You can remove desktop icons by deselecting them here.

Create a shortcut on the desktop for a program or application

Shortcuts you place on the desktop let you access folders, files, programs and other items by double-clicking them. Shortcuts always appear with an arrow beside them (or on them, actually). The easiest way to create a shortcut to a program (or other item) you access often is to locate it and right-click it. To create a shortcut for a program installed on your computer, you'll have to find it in the All Programs menu first, as detailed here.

1 Click Start, then click All Programs.

2 Locate the program you'd like to create a shortcut for and right-click it.

3 Click Send To.

4 Click Desktop (create shortcut).

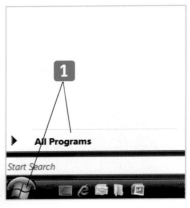

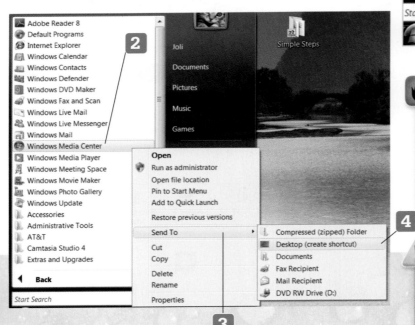

HOT TIP: You can create a shortcut for a file, folder, picture, song or other item by locating it and right-clicking, as detailed in this section.

ALERT: You can delete a shortcut by dragging it to the Recycle Bin. Be careful though: only delete shortcuts – don't delete any actual folders!

Remove icons and shortcuts from the desktop

When you're ready to remove items from the desktop, you'll use the right-click method again. The options you'll have when you right-click an item on the desktop will differ depending on what type of icon you select. You can delete shortcuts and Vista icons like Computer and Network safely, but be careful that you don't delete any actual data you want to keep. Make sure you always read the warning before deleting.

1 Right-click the icon to remove.

2 Click Delete.

3 Read the warning and click Yes to complete the deletion.

HOT TIP: Even if you accidentally delete something you want to keep, you can find it, and restore it, from the Recycle Bin.

ALERT: If you are deleting a shortcut, you might see a warning that you are moving a file to the Recycle Bin, when in reality you are not. Remember, if it has an arrow by it, it's a shortcut and can be deleted.

Open your personal folder

You store the data you want to keep in your personal folder. Your data includes documents, pictures, music, contacts, videos and more. The Start menu offers a place to easily access this folder, as well as installed programs, Vista features and applications (like Windows Mail and Internet Explorer), recent items you've accessed and games, among other things.

1 Click Start.

2 Click your user name.

3 View the items in your personal folder.

> **?** **DID YOU KNOW?**
>
> You can click on anything you see in the Start menu to open it and then close it using the X in the top right corner of the program window. Don't worry – you can't hurt anything!

> **🔥** **HOT TIP:** Double-click any folder inside your personal folder to open it. Click the back arrow to return to the previous view (also called a window).

Close a folder or window

Each time you click an icon in the Start menu, All Programs menu or on the desktop, a window opens to display its contents. The window will stay open until you close it. To close a window, click the X in the top right corner.

1 Click Start.

2 Click your user name. Your personal folder opens.

3 Click the X in the top right corner to close it.

3

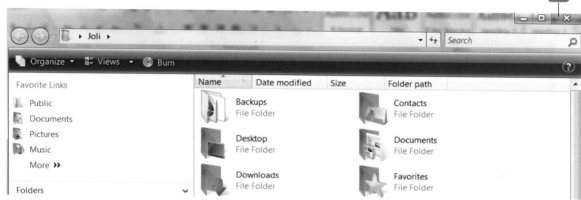

> 🔥 **HOT TIP:** If you don't want to close the window but instead want to simply hide it, click the 'minimise' button. It's the – to the left of the X in the top right corner.

Open an application or program

Programs (also called applications or software) offer computer users, like you, a way to perform tasks such as writing letters or editing photos. You open programs that are installed on your computer from the Start menu. Once a program is open, you can access its tools to perform tasks. For instance, if you open Windows Photo Gallery, you can use the interface options to view photos, fix problems with photos, place photos in categories, rate them and delete them (among other things).

1 Click Start.

2 Click All Programs.

3 If necessary, use the scroll bar to locate Windows Photo Gallery.

4 Click Windows Photo Gallery to open the application.

5 Click the X in the top right corner to close the application.

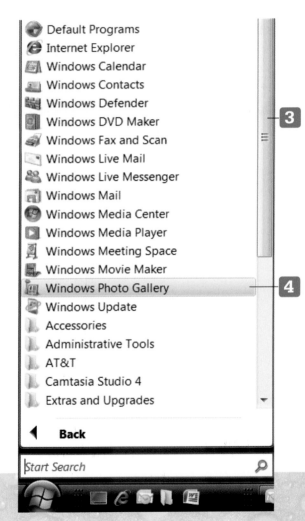

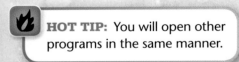

HOT TIP: You will open other programs in the same manner.

? DID YOU KNOW?
To close most programs, you can also click File and then Exit.

Search for a program

To locate a program on your computer you can search for it using the Start Search window. Just type in what you want and select the appropriate program from the list. Note that when you search using the Start Search window, all kinds of results may appear, not just programs. For instance, if you're looking for Windows Photo Gallery and you search for 'photo', you'll see much more than just Windows Photo Gallery in the results. Let's do that so you can get a feel for searching with the Start menu.

1 Click Start.

2 In the Start Search window, type Photo.

3 Note the results.

4 Click any result to open it. If you want to open Windows Photo Gallery, click it once. Note that it's under Programs.

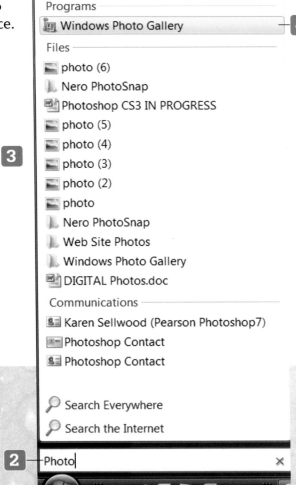

HOT TIP: The easiest way to find something on your computer is to type it into this search window.

Enable the Sidebar

Windows Sidebar is a nifty feature that sits on your desktop and offers information on the weather, time and date, as well as access to your contacts, productivity tools and CPU usage. You can even have a slideshow of your favourite pictures. You can customise the Sidebar by hiding it, keeping it on top of or underneath open windows, adding or removing 'gadgets' and even detaching gadgets from the Sidebar for use anywhere on the desktop.

1 If the sidebar is not on the desktop, click Start.

2 In the Start Search window, type Sidebar.

3 Under Programs, click Windows Sidebar.

ALERT: You won't get up-to-date information on the weather, clock and other real-time gadgets unless you're connected to the Internet.

? DID YOU KNOW?
By default, the Sidebar is enabled. If you can see the Sidebar, skip this section.

Set the time on the clock gadget

Almost all gadgets on the Sidebar offer up a wrench icon when you position your mouse over them. You can use this icon to access settings for the gadget. The first thing you may want to set is the time on the clock gadget.

1 Position the mouse pointer over the clock in the sidebar. Look for the small X and the wrench to appear. Click the wrench by the clock.

Note: Clicking the X will remove the gadget from the Sidebar. Clicking the wrench will open the gadget's properties, if properties are available.

2 Click the arrow in the Time zone window and select your time zone from the list.

3 Click the right arrow underneath the clock to change the clock type.

4 Click OK.

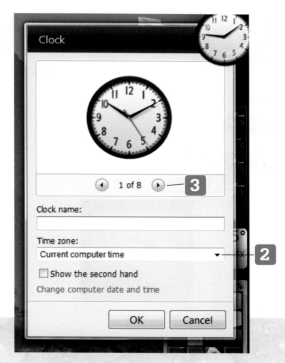

SEE ALSO: The Sidebar must be enabled to access the clock icon. To enable it, refer to the previous section, Enable the Sidebar.

ALERT: The Stocks gadget runs about 15 minutes behind real-time stock data, so don't start buying and selling based on what you see here!

Add or remove a Sidebar gadget

Windows Vista comes with several gadgets in its 'Gadget Gallery', allowing you to add gadgets easily. You can remove gadgets from the Sidebar by clicking the X icon that appears when you hover the mouse over them.

1 To add a gadget, right-click an empty area of the Sidebar.

2 Click Add Gadgets.

3 In the gadget gallery, drag the gadget you want to add to the Sidebar and drop it there. (Repeat as desired.)

4 Click the X in the Gadget Gallery to close it.

5 Click the X in any gadget to remove it from the sidebar. This does not remove it from the computer. Remember the X will not appear until you hover the mouse over it.

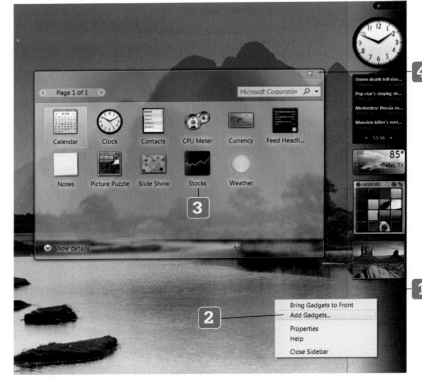

ALERT: Although you can get gadgets online, make sure you read the reviews of the gadgets you want prior to downloading and installing them – they could be buggy or dangerous. Don't be afraid to get gadgets online, just be careful and read the reviews before installing.

? DID YOU KNOW?

Right-click an empty area of the Sidebar and select Properties to change what side of the desktop the Sidebar appears on.

Close the Sidebar

Not everyone likes the Sidebar. If you want to close it, use a right-click.

1 Right-click an empty area of the Sidebar.

2 Click Close Sidebar.

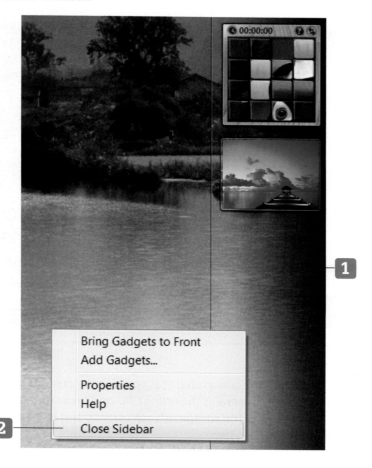

DID YOU KNOW?

You can show the Sidebar by clicking the sidebar icon on the taskbar. The taskbar is the grey bar that runs across the bottom of your screen.

Shut down Windows safely

When you're ready to turn off your computer, you need to do so using the method detailed here. Simply pressing the power button can damage the computer and/or the operating system.

1 Click Start.

2 Click the arrow shown here.

3 Click Shut Down.

WHAT DOES THIS MEAN?

Processor: Short for microprocessor, it's the silicon chip that contains the central processing unit (CPU) inside a computer. Generally, the terms CPU and processor are used interchangeably. The CPU does almost all of the computer's calculations and is the most important piece of hardware in a computer system.

RAM: Short for random access memory, it's the hardware inside your computer that temporarily stores data that is being used by the operating system or programs. Although there are many types of RAM, all you need to know is that the more RAM you have, the faster your computer will (theoretically) run and perform.

GPU: Short for graphics processing unit, it's a processor used specifically for rendering graphics. Having a processor just for graphics frees up the main CPU, allowing it to work faster on other tasks.

GHz: Short for gigahertz, this term describes how fast a processor can work. One GHz equals 1 billion cycles per second, so a 2.4 GHz computer chip will execute calculations at 240 billion cycles per second. Again, it's only important to know that the faster the chip, the faster the PC.

Icon: A visual representation of an application, feature or program.

2 Computing essentials

Introduction

To get the most out of your computer you need to understand some basic computing essentials. For example, it's important to understand what a 'window' is and how to resize, move or arrange open windows on your desktop. All of this is essential because each time you open a program, file, folder, picture or anything else, a new window almost always opens. You have to be very familiar with these windows, including how to show or hide them, in order to become comfortable navigating your computer. Beyond understanding windows though, you'll need to know how to get help when you need it, using Help and Support, and how to watch the demonstration videos that come with Windows Vista.

Change the view in the Pictures window

When you open your personal folder from the Start menu, you will see additional folders inside it. These folders include Documents, Pictures, and Music, among

others. You'll use these subfolders to organise the data you create and save, such as documents, pictures, songs and similar data. You open a folder to see what's in it. You can change what the content inside these folders looks like though. You can configure each folder independently so that the data appear in a list, as small icons or as large icons, to name a few.

1 Click Start.

2 Click Pictures.

3 Click the arrow next to views.

4 Move the slider to select an option from the list.

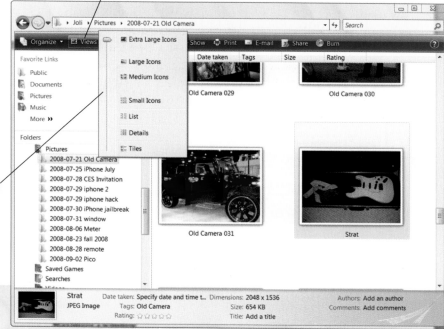

HOT TIP: Show items in the Pictures folder as large or extra large icons and you'll be able to tell what each picture looks like without actually opening it in a program.

HOT TIP: Show items in the Documents window as Details to see the name of each document as well as the date it was created.

Minimise a window

When you have several open windows, you may want to minimise (hide) the windows you aren't using. A minimised window appears on the taskbar as a small icon and is not on the desktop. When you're ready to use the window again, you simply click it.

1 Open any window. (Click Start, then click Pictures, Documents, Games or any other option.)

2 Click the (–) sign in the top right corner.

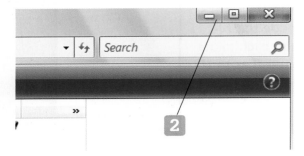

3 Locate the window title in the taskbar. Position your mouse over the icon to see its thumbnail.

ALERT: A minimised window is on the taskbar and is not shown on the desktop. You can 'restore' the window by clicking on its icon on the taskbar. Restoring a window to the desktop brings the window back up so that you can work with it.

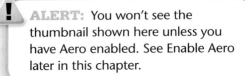

ALERT: You won't see the thumbnail shown here unless you have Aero enabled. See Enable Aero later in this chapter.

Restore a window

A window can be minimised (on the taskbar), maximised (filling the entire desktop) or in restore mode (not maximised or minimised, but showing on the desktop). When a window is in restore mode, you can resize or move the window as desired. You cannot resize or move windows that are minimised or maximised.

In order to put a window in restore mode, you have to have access to the restore button. The restore button is made up of two squares that appear next to the X in the top right corner of any window. Clicking this button will put the window in restore mode. Once it is in restore mode, you can resize or move the window. If the icon next to the X in the top right corner of a window is a single square, the window is already in restore mode and the only thing you can do is minimise or maximise it.

1 Open a window.

2 In the top right corner of the window, locate the two square buttons.

3 Click the button to put the window in restore mode.

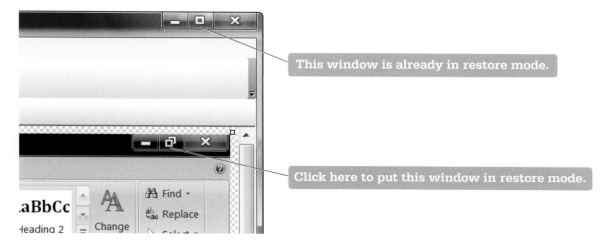

This window is already in restore mode.

Click here to put this window in restore mode.

ALERT: Remember, if you don't see two squares but instead see only one, the window is already in restore mode.

Maximise a window

A maximized window is as large as it can be and takes up the entire screen. You can maximise a window that is on the desktop by clicking the square icon in the top right corner. If the icon is already two squares, it's already maximised.

1 Open a window.

2 In the top right corner of the window, locate the square.

3 Click it to maximise the window.

4 When a window is maximised and taking up the entire screen, you can still access the other windows from the Taskbar.

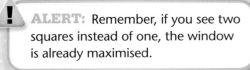

ALERT: Remember, if you see two squares instead of one, the window is already maximised.

Move a window

You can move a window as long as it's in restore mode. You move a window by dragging it from its title bar. The title bar is the bar that runs across the top of the window. Moving windows allows you to position multiple windows across the screen.

1 Open any window.

2 Put the window in restore mode if it is not already.

3 Left-click with the mouse on the title bar and drag. Let go of the mouse when the window is positioned correctly.

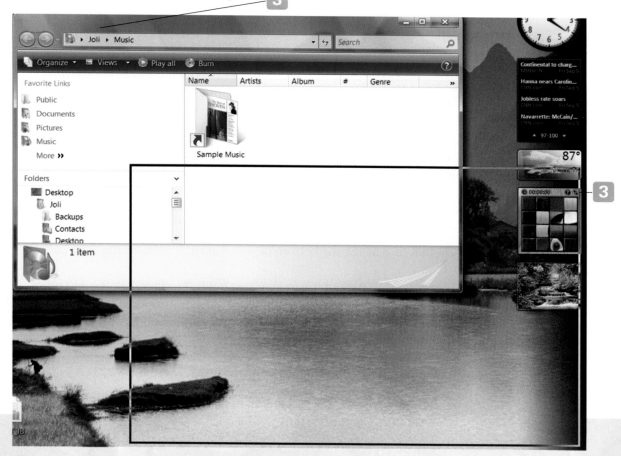

? **DID YOU KNOW?**

You can open a document or a picture and it will open in a window.

Resize a window

Resizing a window allows you to change the dimensions of the window. You can resize a window by dragging from its sides, corners or the top and bottom.

1 Open any window. (If you're unsure, click Start and Pictures.)

2 Put the window in restore mode. You want the maximise button to show.

3 Position the mouse at one of the window corners, so that the mouse pointer becomes a two-pointed arrow.

ALERT: You can move and resize windows only if they are in restore mode, meaning the maximise button is showing in the top right corner of the window.

4 Hold down the mouse button and drag the arrow to resize the window.

5 Repeat as desired, dragging from the sides, top, bottom or corners.

WHAT DOES THIS MEAN?

Taskbar: The grey bar that runs across the bottom of your screen. It contains the Start button and the Notification area.

Notification area: The far right portion of the taskbar that holds the clock, volume and other system icons.

Windows Media Center: A program that is included with Windows Vista for viewing videos, listening to music and viewing pictures.

Enable Aero

Aero is an interface enhancement you can enable for a cleaner, sleeker interface and Vista experience. You can use Aero only if your computer hardware supports it, meaning that the hardware installed on your computer meets Aero's minimum requirements and that you are running something other than Windows Vista Basic (i.e. Home Premium, Ultimate or Business). Windows Aero builds on the basic Windows Vista interface and offers a high-performing desktop experience that includes (among other things) the translucent effect of Aero Glass. Aero Glass offers visual reflections and soft animations too, making the interface quite 'comfortable'.

Instead of spelling out what is actually required to run Windows Aero, let's just see whether you can enable it. If you can, your hardware supports it, if you can't, it doesn't. Once enabled, you'll learn how to use Flip and Flip 3D.

1 Right-click an empty area of the desktop.

2 Click Personalize.

3 Click Window Color and Appearance.

Tasks

Change desktop icons

Adjust font size (DPI)

Personalize appearance and sounds

Window Color and Appearance
Fine tune the color and style of your windows.

Desktop Background
Choose from available backgrounds or colors or use one of your own pictures to decorate the desktop.

Screen Saver
Change your screen saver or adjust when it displays. A screen saver is a picture or animation that covers your screen and appears when your computer is idle for a set period of time.

? DID YOU KNOW?
You don't have to use Aero. If you prefer the basic Vista experience, you can turn this feature off.

! ALERT: You don't have to do anything if Aero is already enabled.

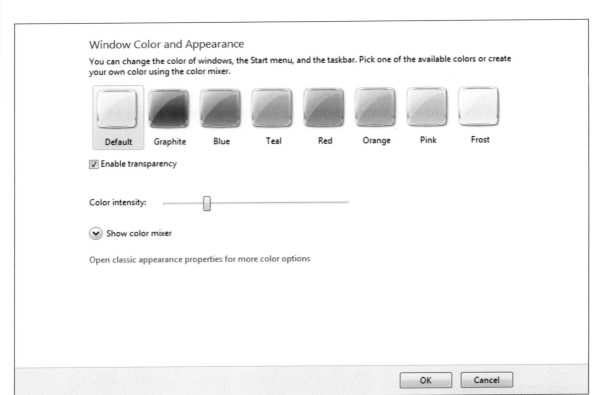

Window Color and Appearance

You can change the color of windows, the Start menu, and the taskbar. Pick one of the available colors or create your own color using the color mixer.

Default   Graphite   Blue   Teal   Red   Orange   Pink   Frost

☑ Enable transparency

Color intensity:

⌄ Show color mixer

Open classic appearance properties for more color options

OK   Cancel

4 If you're not using Aero already, you'll see the Appearance Settings dialogue box. If you're currently using Windows Aero, you'll see the Aero options, shown here.

5 To change from Windows Vista Basic to Windows Aero, click Windows Aero in the Color scheme options, then click OK.

Appearance Settings

Appearance

Inactive Window

Active Window

Window Text

Message Box

OK

Color scheme:

Windows Aero
Windows Vista Basic
Windows Standard
Windows Classic
High Contrast White
High Contrast Black
High Contrast #2

Effects...

Advanced...

OK   Cancel   Apply

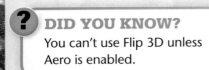

? DID YOU KNOW?

You can't use Flip 3D unless Aero is enabled.

Use Flip

Windows Flip offers a quick way to choose a specific window when multiple windows are open. With Flip, you can scroll through open windows until you land on the one you want to use, then select it.

1 With multiple windows open, on the keyboard hold down the Alt key with one finger (or thumb).

2 Press and hold the Tab key.

3 Press the Tab key again (making sure that the Alt key is still depressed).

4 When the item you want to bring to the front is selected, let go of the Tab key, then let go of the Alt key.

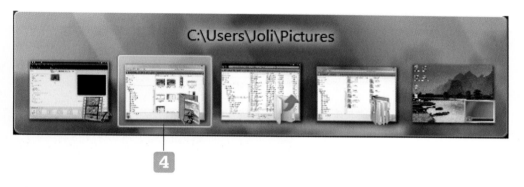

C:\Users\Joli\Pictures

4

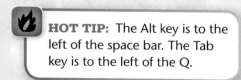

HOT TIP: The Alt key is to the left of the space bar. The Tab key is to the left of the Q.

Use Flip 3D

Windows Flip 3D offers a quick way to choose a specific window when multiple windows are open. With Flip 3D, you can scroll through open windows until you land on the one you want to use, then select it.

1 With multiple windows open, on the keyboard, hold down the Windows key (which may have Start written on it) with one finger (or thumb).

2 Click the Tab key once while keeping the Alt key depressed.

3 Press the Tab key again (making sure that the Alt key is still depressed) to scroll through the open windows.

4 When the item you want to bring to the front is selected, let go of the Tab key, then let go of the Alt key.

HOT TIP: The Windows key is the key to the left of the Alt key and has the Windows logo printed on it.

ALERT: If Flip 3D doesn't work, or if you get only Flip and not Flip 3D, either your PC does not support Aero or it is not configured to use it.

Use Help and Support

Sometimes you need a little bit more than a book can give you. When that happens, you'll need to access Windows Vista's Help and Support feature. You can access Help and Support from the Start menu.

1 Click Start.

2 Click Help and Support.

3 Select any topic to read more about it.

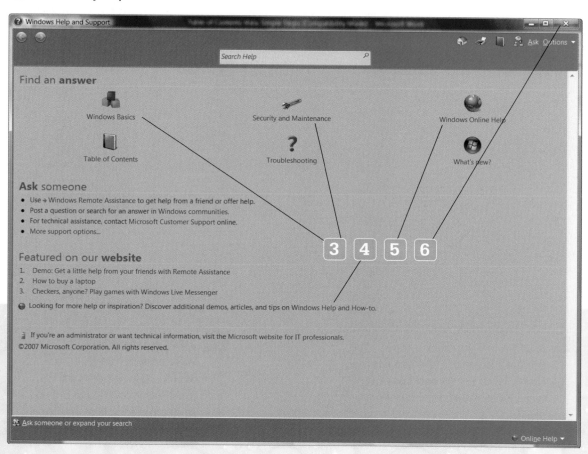

4 To view demos, articles and tips, click Windows Help and How-To.

5 To get help from online sources, click Windows Online Help.

6 Click the X in the top right of the Help and Support Center to close it.

? DID YOU KNOW?
If you're looking for something in particular, click Table of Contents. From the Contents page, just click the option that most closely matches what you're looking for.

HOT TIP: You can access the Help and Support Center from virtually anywhere in Windows Vista. Look for the round blue question mark.

! ALERT: If you click a topic, click the Back button in the top left corner of the Help and Support window to return to the previous screen.

 DID YOU KNOW?
You can type words in the Search Help window and press Enter on the keyboard to perform a search of any topic.

Watch demonstration videos

Windows Vista offers demonstration videos. You may be interested in watching the videos regarding the 'basics'. These video demonstrations show you how to use the mouse, use the desktop, print, work with files, use the web (Internet) and more.

1 Open the Welcome Center and under Get started with Windows, click Show all ___ items...

2 Double-click Windows Vista Demos.

3 Click Watch the demo to watch it.

4 To stop the demo, or to close Windows Media Player, click the X in Windows Media Player.

? DID YOU KNOW?
The Welcome Center can be found by typing Welcome Center in the Start search window.

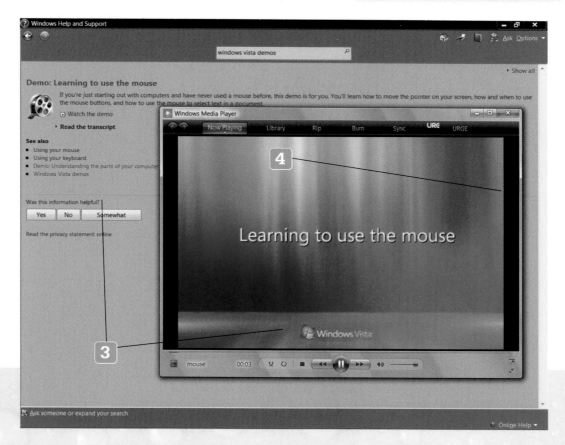

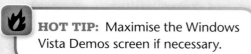 **HOT TIP:** Maximise the Windows Vista Demos screen if necessary.

 ALERT: You may need to turn up your speakers to hear the demo!

3 Perform tasks with Windows Vista

Introduction

Windows comes with a lot of applications, many of which may sound familiar, like WordPad and Calculator, and some of which may not, like the Snipping Tool and the Sound Recorder. These applications, like so many others, can help you complete everyday tasks like writing and printing a letter, balancing your cheque book, taking a picture of the screen or recording a sound bite. There are games too, and tools to keep your computer running smoothly like Disk Cleanup and Disk Defragmenter.

In this chapter you'll explore these features. You'll learn how to write and print a letter, for instance, and access and use accessories like the Calculator and the Snipping Tool. You'll even learn to play a game of Solitaire on the computer.

Write a letter with Notepad

If your word-processing tasks involve only creating a quick memo, note or letter and printing it out, or putting together a weekly newsletter that you send via email, there's no reason to purchase a large office suite like Microsoft Office (and learn how to use it) when Notepad will do just fine. You can't create and insert tables, add endnotes, add text boxes or perform similar tasks with Notepad, but you may not need to. Notepad is a simple program with only a few features, making it easy to learn and use.

1 Click Start.

2 In the Start Search window, type Notepad.

3 Click Notepad under Programs. (Note that you may see other results, as shown here.)

4 Click once inside Notepad and start typing.

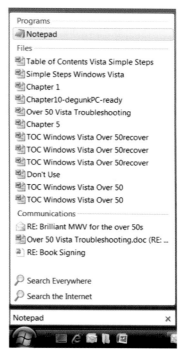

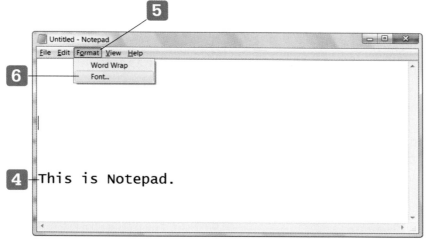

5 To change the font or font size, select the typed text and click Format.

6 Click Font.

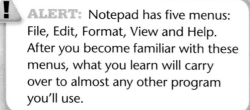

ALERT: Notepad has five menus: File, Edit, Format, View and Help. After you become familiar with these menus, what you learn will carry over to almost any other program you'll use.

DID YOU KNOW?

The Format menu includes options for setting the font, font style, font size and more.

7 Use the scroll bar to locate a font. Select the font you like.

8 Select a font style.

9 Select a font size.

10 Click OK.

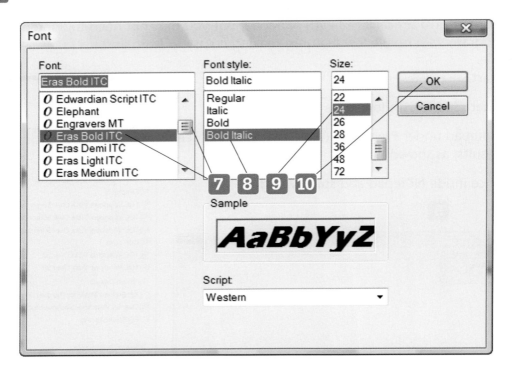

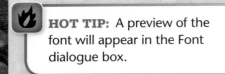 **HOT TIP:** A preview of the font will appear in the Font dialogue box.

ALERT: If you close Notepad before saving the file, your work will be lost!

Save a letter with Notepad

If you want to save a letter you've written in Notepad, you have to click File and then Save. This will allow you to name the file and save it to your hard drive. The next time you want to view the file, you can click File and then click Open. You'll be able to locate and open your saved file using the same technique you used to save it. You can reopen a saved file and make changes to it, then resave it. Your changes will be saved as well.

1 Click File.

2 Click Save.

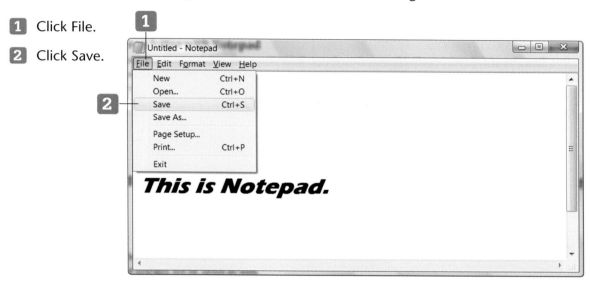

3 Type a name for the file.

4 Click Save.

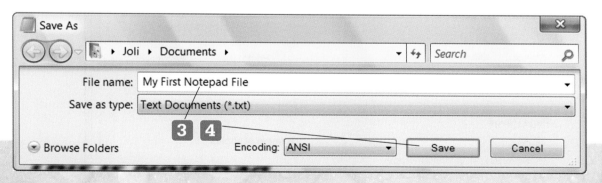

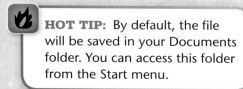 **HOT TIP:** By default, the file will be saved in your Documents folder. You can access this folder from the Start menu.

Print a letter with Notepad

Sometimes you'll need to print a letter so you can mail it. You can access the Print command from the File menu.

1 Click File.

2 Click Print.

3 Select a printer.

4 Click Print.

HOT TIP: You have to have a printer installed, plugged in and turned on to print.

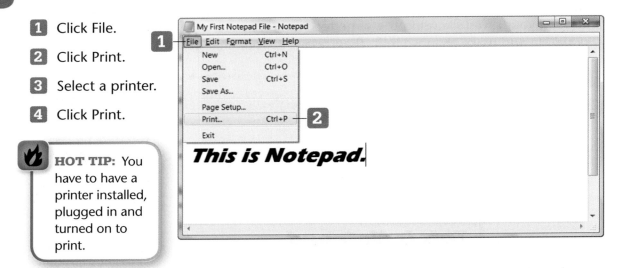

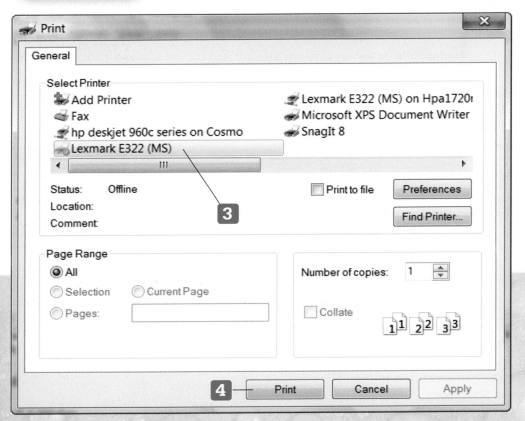

Use the calculator

You've probably used a calculator before and using Vista's calculator is not much different from a hand-held one, except that you input numbers with a mouse click, keyboard or number pad. There are two calculator options: Standard and Scientific. The Standard calculator is the default and is a bare-bones version. The Scientific calculator offers many more features.

1 Click Start.

2 In the Start Search dialogue box, type Calculator.

3 In the Programs results, click Calculator.

4 Input numbers using the keypad or by clicking the on-screen calculator with the mouse.

5 Input operations using the keypad or input numbers by clicking the on-screen calculator with the mouse.

6 Close Calculator by clicking the X in the top right corner.

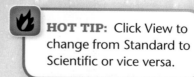

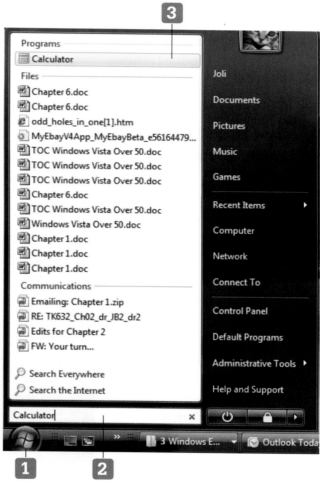

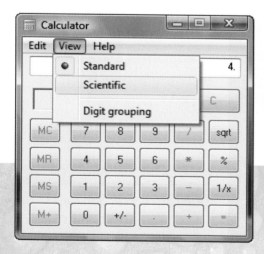

HOT TIP: Click View to change from Standard to Scientific or vice versa.

Take a screen shot

The Snipping Tool lets you drag your mouse cursor around any area on the screen to copy and capture it. Once captured, you can save it, edit it and/or send it to an email recipient. There are several ways to edit the 'clip' or 'snip' (either one will do for a name for the copied data); you can start by copying it or writing on it using a variety of tools. (These tools will become available after creating a snip.) You can write on a clip with a red, blue, black or customised pen or a highlighter and if you mess up, you can use the eraser.

1 Click Start.

2 In the Start Search dialogue box, type Snip.

3 Under Programs, select Snipping Tool.

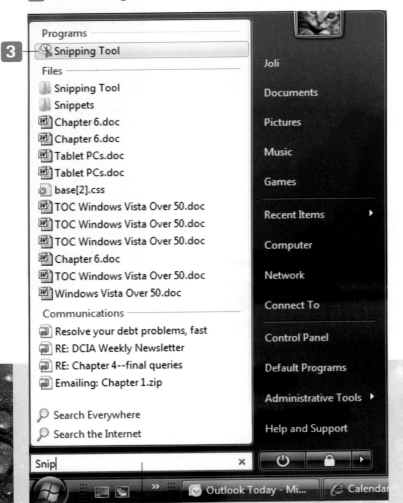

HOT TIP: You can take a screen shot of a webpage, document, presentation or anything else showing on your screen.

4 Drag your mouse across any part of the screen. When you let go of the mouse, the snip will appear in the Snipping Tool window.

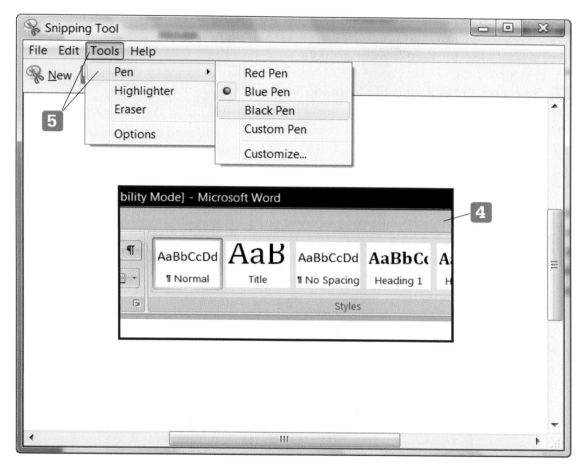

5 Click Tools, and click Pen, to access the pen options. You can use the pen to draw on the snip.

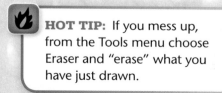 **HOT TIP:** If you mess up, from the Tools menu choose Eraser and "erase" what you have just drawn.

ALERT: If you want to keep the snip you'll have to save it. Click File and click Save As to name the file and save it to your hard drive.

Email a screen shot

You can use the Snipping Tool to take a picture of your screen as detailed in the previous section. You can even write on it with a 'pen'. You can also email that screen shot if you'd like to share it with someone.

1 Take a screen shot with the Snipping Tool.

2 Click File and click Send To.

3 Click E-mail Recipient.

4 Insert the recipient's name, change the subject if desired type a message if desired and click Send.

ALERT: If you select Email Recipient, this will insert the snip inside an email. Note that you can also send the snip as an attachment.

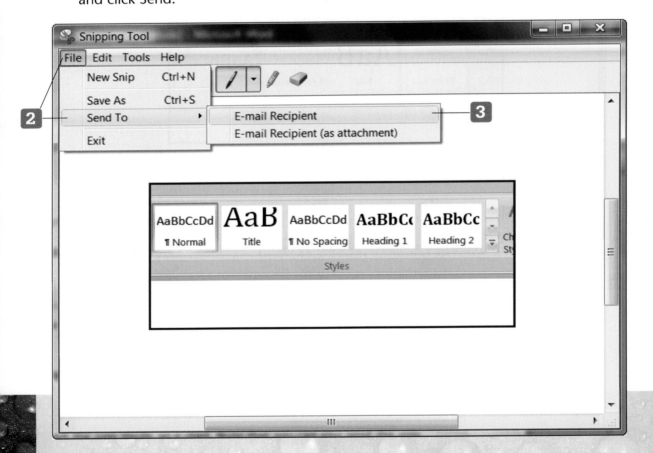

SEE ALSO: For more information on sending an email, refer to Chapter 6.

HOT TIP: Emails you send can be viewed in Mail's 'Sent' folder.

Play Solitaire

Windows Vista comes with lots of games. You access the available games from the Games folder on the Start menu. Each game offers instructions on how to play it, and for the most part moving a player, tile or card, dealing a card, or otherwise moving around the screen is performed using the mouse. One of the most popular games is Solitaire.

1 Click Start.

2 Click Games.

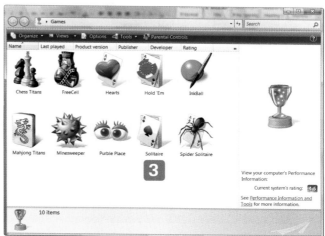

3 Double-click Solitaire to begin the game.

4 Double-click any card to move it or drag the card to the desired location.

 HOT TIP: Instructions will appear on the screen and you can also access instructions from the Help menu.

Record a sound clip

Need to record a quick note to yourself, a music clip, a sound or other audible? It's easy with Sound Recorder. Sound Recorder is a simple tool with only three options: Start Recording, Stop Recording and Resume Recording. To record, click Start Recording; to stop, click Stop Recording; to continue, click Resume Recording. You save your recording as a Windows Media Audio file, which will play by default in Windows Media Player.

1 Click Start.

2 In the Start Search dialogue box, click Sound Recorder.

3 Under Programs, click Sound Recorder.

4 Click Start Recording and speak into your microphone.

 HOT TIP: You can use your saved recording in Movie Maker and other Vista-related programs, and you can save and play the clip on your iPod or other media player.

5 Click Stop Recording to complete the recording.

 **ALERT:** You can't record anything without a microphone.

6 In the Save As dialogue box, type a name for your recording.

7 Click Save.

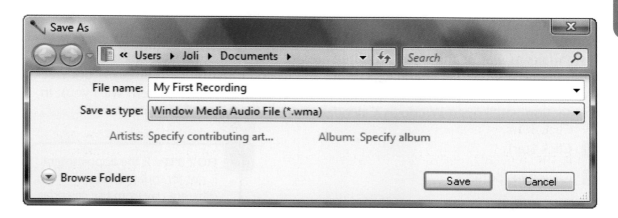

8 Click the X in the Sound Recorder to close it.

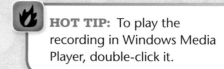

ALERT: To locate your file, open your Documents folder. It might be on the desktop, but you can always find it on the Start menu.

HOT TIP: To play the recording in Windows Media Player, double-click it.

Create an appointment in Windows Calendar

Windows Calendar is a full-featured calendar application that lets you manage your own affairs as well as the affairs of others, using a familiar calendar interface. You can easily create appointments and tasks, view the calendar by the current day, work week, week or month, and you can share your calendar with others (and them with you). In this section you'll open Windows Calendar and create an appointment.

1 Click Start.

2 Click All Programs.

3 Click Windows Calendar.

4 Click New Appointment.

5 Type a name for the new appointment.

6 Set the start and end time.

7 Set a reminder.

8 Close Windows Calendar.

 HOT TIP: If the appointment is not for today, select a different day from the calendar shown in the top left corner of Windows Calendar.

 HOT TIP: You can use the arrows to set the time, choose a reminder and access other drop-down menus.

? **DID YOU KNOW?**
Remember, to close a window, click the X in the top right corner. If you're prompted to save, do so.

Use Disk Cleanup

Disk Cleanup is a safe and effective way to reduce unnecessary data on your PC. With unnecessary data deleted, your PC will run faster and have more available disk space for saving files and installing programs. With Disk Cleanup you can remove temporary files, empty the Recycle Bin, remove set-up log files and downloaded program files (among other things), all in a single process.

1 Click Start.

2 In the Start Search dialogue box, type Disk Cleanup.

3 In the results, under Programs, click Disk Cleanup.

4 Choose My files only to clean your files and nothing else. Choose Files from all users on this computer if you wish to clean additional users' files.

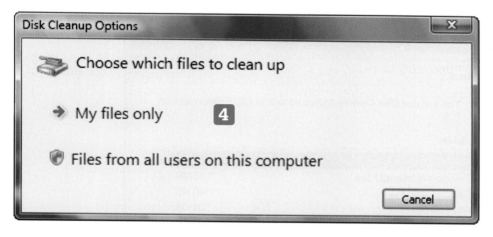

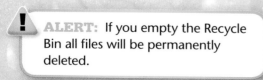

ALERT: If you empty the Recycle Bin all files will be permanently deleted.

5 If prompted to choose a drive or partition, choose the letter of the drive that contains the operating system, which is almost always C, but occasionally D. Click OK.

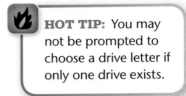

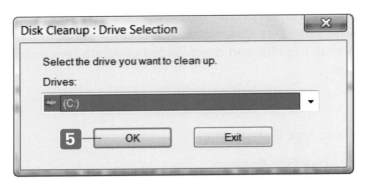

6 Select the files to delete. Accept the defaults if you aren't sure.

7 Click OK to start the cleaning process.

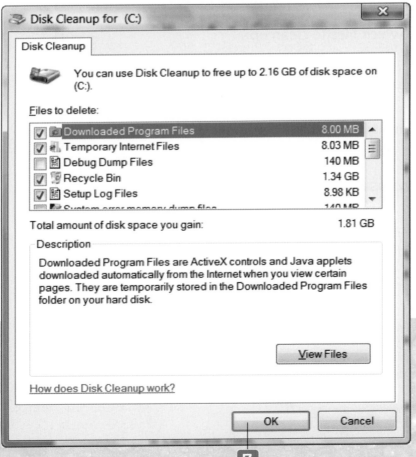

Use Disk Defragmenter

A hard drive stores the files and data on your computer. When you want to access a file, the hard drive spins and data are accessed from the drive. When the data required for the file you need are all in one place, they are accessed more quickly than if that data are scattered across the hard drive in different areas. When data are scattered, they are fragmented.

1 Click Start.

2 In the Start Search dialogue box, type Defrag.

3 Under Programs, select Disk Defragmenter.

4 Verify that Disk Defragmenter is configured to run on a schedule. If not, place a tick in the appropriate box.

5 To manually run Disk Defragmenter, click Defragment now.

6 Click OK.

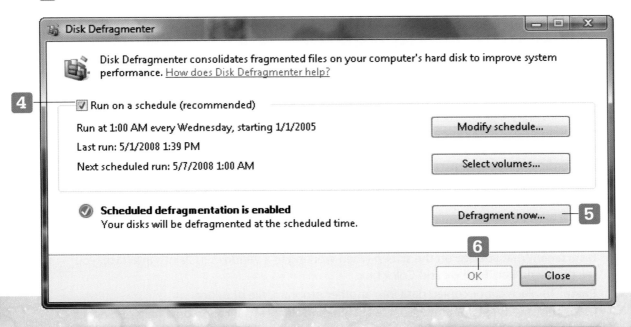

? DID YOU KNOW?

Disk Defragmenter analyses the data stored on your hard drive and consolidates files that are not stored together.

? DID YOU KNOW?

By default, Disk Defragmenter runs automatically and on a schedule, but it is best to verify this.

WHAT DOES THIS MEAN?

Menu bar: The bar that runs across the top of Notepad with the menus File, Edit, View, Insert, Format and Help.

File menu: Lets you open, save, close and print files.

Edit menu: Lets you edit text you've written using cut, copy and paste, among other features.

Printer Preferences: Lets you select the page orientation, print order and type of paper you'll be printing on, among other features.

Page Range: Lets you select what pages to print.

Downloaded program files: These are files that download automatically when you view certain webpages. They are stored temporarily in a folder on your hard disk and accessed when and if needed.

Temporary Internet files: These files contain copies of webpages you've visited on your hard drive, so that you can view the pages more quickly when visiting the pages again.

Offline webpages: These are webpages that you've chosen to store on your computer so you can view them without being connected to the Internet. Upon connection, the data are synchronised.

Recycle Bin: This contains files you've deleted. Files are not permanently deleted until you empty the Recycle Bin.

Setup log files: Files created by Windows during set-up processes.

Temporary files: Files created and stored by programs for use by the program. Most of these temporary files are deleted when you exit the program, but some do remain.

Thumbnails: These are small icons of your pictures, videos and documents. Thumbnails will be recreated as needed, even if you delete them here.

Per user archived Windows Error Reporting: Files used for error reporting and solution checking.

System archived Windows Error Reporting: Files used for error reporting and solution checking.

Copy: To copy the selected text, picture or object

Clipboard: An imaginary 'clipboard' where data you cut are stored until you paste them, reboot your PC or cut something else.

Cut: To remove the selected text, picture or object and place the item on the clipboard.

Interface: What you see on the screen when working in a window. In Paint's interface, you see the Menu bar, Toolbox and Color box.

Paste: To place cut or copied data into another program, file or folder.

URL: This stands for Uniform Resource Locator and denotes a location on a network, either the Internet or a local network.

4 Files and folders

Introduction

You're going to have data to save. That data may come in the form of letters you type on the computer, pictures you take using your digital camera, music you copy from your CD collection, email address books, videos from a DV camera, holiday card and gift lists, and more. Each time you click the Save or Save As button under a file menu (which is what you do to save data to your PC most of the time), you'll be prompted to tell Vista *where* you want to save the data. For the most part though, Vista will *tell you* where it thinks you should save the data. Documents go in the Documents folder, music in the Music folder, pictures in the Pictures folder and so on.

In this chapter you'll learn where files are saved by default and how to create your own folders and subfolders for organising data. You'll also learn how to copy, move and delete files and folders, how to locate saved files in various ways and how to perform searches for data and save the search results for later use.

Create a folder

Microsoft understands what type of data you want to save to your computer and built Vista's folder structure based on that information. Look at the Start menu. You'll see your name at the top. Clicking your name on the Start menu opens your personal folder.

While Vista's default folders will suit your needs for a while, it won't last. Soon you'll need to create subfolders inside those folders to manage your data and keep it organised. You may also want to create a folder on the desktop to hold information you access often.

1 Right-click an empty area of your desktop.

2 Point to New.

3 Click Folder.

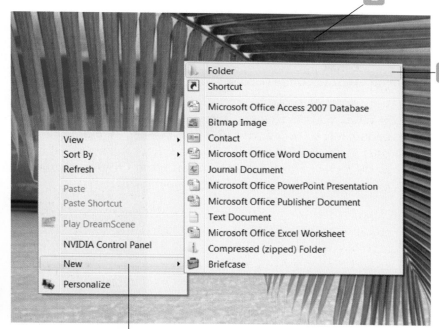

4 Type a name for the folder.

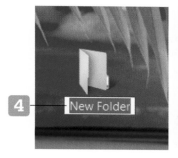

5 Press Enter on the keyboard.

ALERT: If you can't type a name for the folder, right-click the folder and select Rename.

HOT TIP: Create a folder to hold data related to a hobby, tax information, work or family.

DID YOU KNOW?
You can drag the folder to another area of the desktop or even to another area of the hard drive to move it there.

Create a subfolder

You can also create folders inside other folders. For instance, inside the Documents folder, you may want to create a subfolder called Tax Information to hold scanned receipts, tax records and account information. Inside the Pictures folder you might create folders named 2009, 2010, or Weddings, Holidays, Grandkids and so on. And in the Saved Games folder you might create subfolders named My Games, My Grandkids' Games or Downloaded Games.

1 Click Start.

2 Click your user name to open your personal folder.

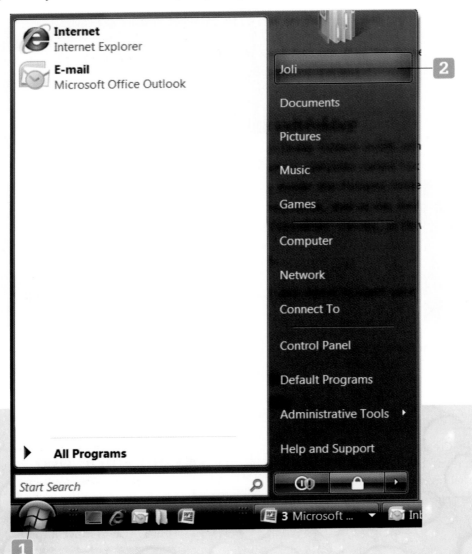

3 Right-click an empty area inside the folder.

4 Point to New.

5 Click Folder.

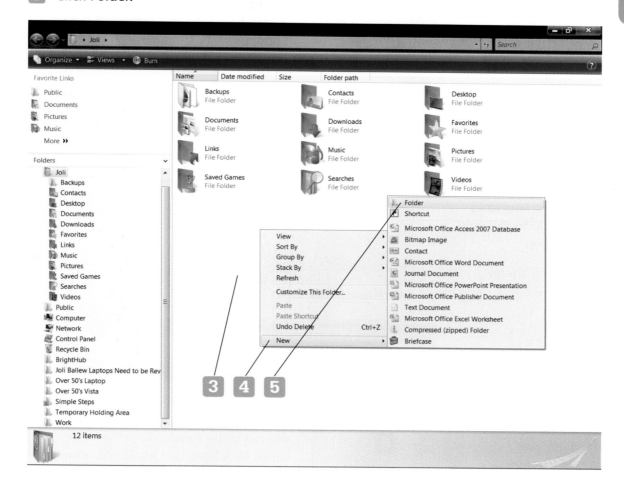

6 Type a name for the folder.

7 Press Enter on the keyboard.

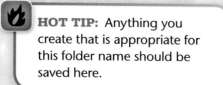

HOT TIP: Anything you create that is appropriate for this folder name should be saved here.

ALERT: If you can't type a name for the folder, right-click the folder and select Rename.

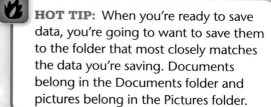

HOT TIP: When you're ready to save data, you're going to want to save them to the folder that most closely matches the data you're saving. Documents belong in the Documents folder and pictures belong in the Pictures folder.

Copy a file

Folders contain files. Files can be documents, pictures, music, videos and more. Sometimes you'll need to copy a file to another location. Perhaps you want to copy the files to an external drive, memory card or USB thumb drive for the purpose of backing them up, or maybe you want to create a copy so you can edit the data in it without worrying about changing the originals. You can find files in your personal folders.

1 Locate a file to copy.

2 Right-click the file.

3 While holding down the right mouse key, drag the file to the new location.

4 Drop it there.

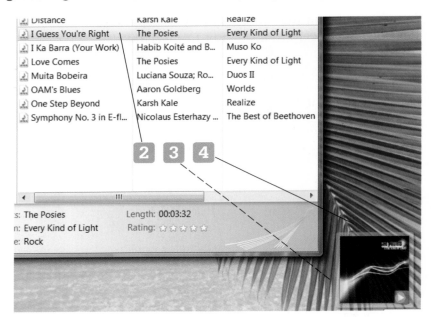

5 Choose Copy Here.

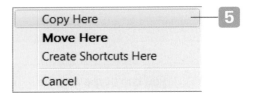

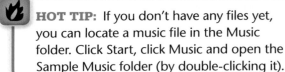

HOT TIP: If you don't have any files yet, you can locate a music file in the Music folder. Click Start, click Music and open the Sample Music folder (by double-clicking it).

? DID YOU KNOW?

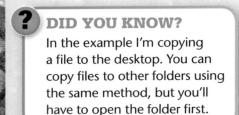

In the example I'm copying a file to the desktop. You can copy files to other folders using the same method, but you'll have to open the folder first.

! ALERT: To delete the copy, right-click it and choose Delete.

Move a file

When you copy something, an exact duplicate is made. The original copy of the data remains where it is and a copy of it is placed somewhere else. For the most part, this is not what you want to do when organising data. When organising data, you generally want to move the data. If a picture of a graduation needs to be put in the Graduation Pictures folder, you need to move it, not copy it.

You move a file in the same way as you copy one, except that when you drop the file you choose Move Here instead of Copy Here.

1 Locate a file to move.

2 Right-click the file.

3 While holding down the right mouse key, drag the file to the new location.

4 Drop it there.

5 Choose Move Here.

 HOT TIP: If you don't have any files yet, you can locate a picture file in the Pictures folder. Click Start, click Pictures, and open the Sample Pictures folder (by double-clicking it).

Forest Flowers   Frangipani Flowers   Garden

 DID YOU KNOW?
In the example I'm moving a file to the desktop. You can move files to other folders using the same method, but you'll have to open the folder first.

HOT TIP: To put the file back in its original location, repeat these steps dragging the file from the desktop back to the Sample Pictures folder.

Delete a file

When you are sure you no longer need a particular file, you can delete it. Deleting it sends the file to the Recycle Bin. This file can be 'restored' if you decide you need the file later, provided you have not emptied the Recycle Bin since deleting it.

1 Locate a file to delete.

2 Right-click the file.

3 Choose Delete.

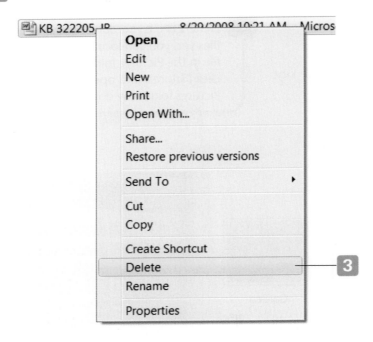

? DID YOU KNOW?

It's best to keep unwanted or unnecessary data off your hard drive. That means you should delete data you don't need, including items in the Recycle Bin.

Copy a folder

Folders often contain other folders. Folders contain files including documents, pictures, music, videos and more. Sometimes you'll need to copy a folder to another location. Perhaps you want to copy the folder to an external drive, memory card or USB thumb drive for the purpose of backing it up, or maybe you want to create a copy so you can edit the data in it without worrying about changing the original. You can find folders in your personal folders.

1 Locate a folder to copy.

> **HOT TIP:** If you don't have any folders yet, you can copy the Sample Pictures folder.

2 Right-click the folder.

3 While holding down the right mouse key, drag the folder to the new location.

4 Drop it there.

5 Choose Copy Here.

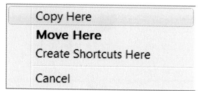

> Copy Here
> **Move Here**
> Create Shortcuts Here
>
> Cancel

> **? DID YOU KNOW?**
> In the example I'm copying a folder to the desktop. You can copy folders to other folders using the same method, but you'll have to open the folder first.

> **! ALERT:** To delete the copy, right-click it and choose Delete.

> **! ALERT:** When you copy a folder, you copy all of the data inside it.

Sample Pictures

: 5/15/2008 9:26 AM
: Everyone

> **? DID YOU KNOW?**
> When you delete a copy of a folder, the original folder remains intact.

Move a folder

When you copy something, an exact duplicate is made. The original copy of the data remains where it is and a copy of it is placed somewhere else. For the most part, this is not what you want to do when organising data. When organising data, you generally want to move the data. If you created a folder called Work on your desktop, for instance, you may want to move the folder (and all its contents) to the inside of your personal folder.

You move a file in the same way that you copy one, except that when you drop the file you choose Move Here instead of Copy Here.

DID YOU KNOW?

You may have to open a folder to locate the folder you want to move.

1 Locate a folder to move.

2 Open the folder you want to move it to. (For instance, open your personal folder by clicking your name on the Start menu.)

3 Right-click the folder.

4 While holding down the right mouse key, drag the file to the new location.

5 Drop it there.

6 Choose Move Here.

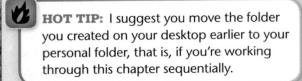

HOT TIP: I suggest you move the folder you created on your desktop earlier to your personal folder, that is, if you're working through this chapter sequentially.

HOT TIP: To put the file back in its original location, repeat these steps, dragging the file from the desktop back to the original location.

Delete a folder

When you are sure you no longer need a particular folder, you can delete it. When you delete a folder you delete the folder and everything in it. Deleting it sends the folder and its contents to the Recycle Bin. This folder can be 'restored' if you decide you need it later, provided you have not emptied the Recycle Bin since deleting it.

1 Locate a folder to delete.

2 Right-click the folder.

3 Choose Delete.

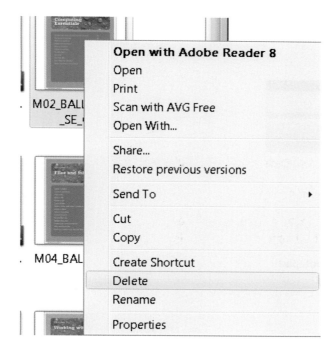

 HOT TIP: If you delete something you find you later need, you can restore it from the Recycle Bin, provided you have not emptied the Recycle Bin since the deletion.

 HOT TIP: You can select a folder with a single click and press the Delete key on the keyboard to delete a folder too.

Open a saved file

If you recall, a file can be a document, picture, song, video, presentation, database or other item. You can create documents in Notepad, upload photos from a digital camera, purchase music online and perform other tasks to obtain data. Once data (in this case, a file) is saved to your hard drive, you can access it, open it and often modify it. Most of the time, you open a saved file from a personal folder or a folder you've created.

1 Click Start.

2 Click Documents.

3 Locate the file to open in the Documents folder.

4 Double-click it to open it.

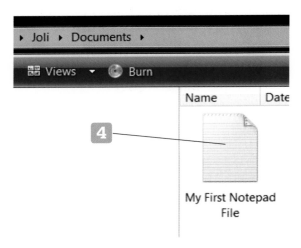

SEE ALSO: Review Write a letter with Notepad and Save a letter with Notepad in Chapter 3 to learn how to create and save a text file.

DID YOU KNOW?
The file will open in the appropriate program automatically.

Search for a file

After you create data, like a Notepad document, you save it to your hard drive. When you're ready to use the file again, you have to locate it and open it. There are several ways to locate a saved file. If you know the document is in the Documents folder, you can click Start, then click Documents. Then, you can simply double-click the file to open it. However, if you aren't sure where the file is, you can search for it from the Start menu.

1 Click Start.

2 In the Start Search window, type the name of the file.

3 Click the file to open it. There will be multiple search results.

> **!** **ALERT:** If you don't know the exact name of the file, you can type part of the name.

> **?** **DID YOU KNOW?**
> If you don't know any part of the name of the file, you can type a word that is included inside the file or a specific type of file.

Browse for a file

Sometimes you'll open a program first and then open a file associated with it. For instance, you may open Notepad and then open a text file using the File>Open command. After clicking Open, you'll then "browse" for the file you want. Browsing is the process of locating a file by looking through the available folders on your hard drive from inside an open program.

1 Open Notepad.

2 Click File and click Open.

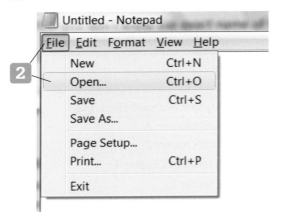

> ▶ **SEE ALSO:** Write a letter with Notepad and Save a letter with Notepad in Chapter 3.

3 Double-click the file to open. If you do not see the file, proceed to Step 4.

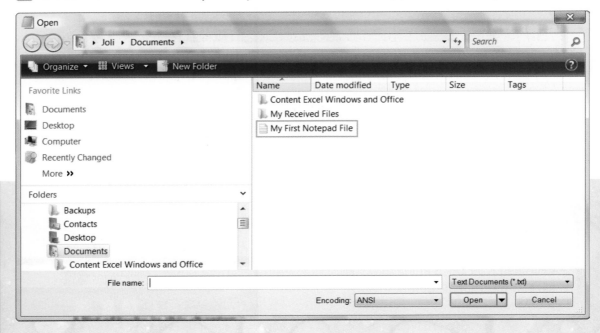

4 Resize the window so that you can see all of the panes.

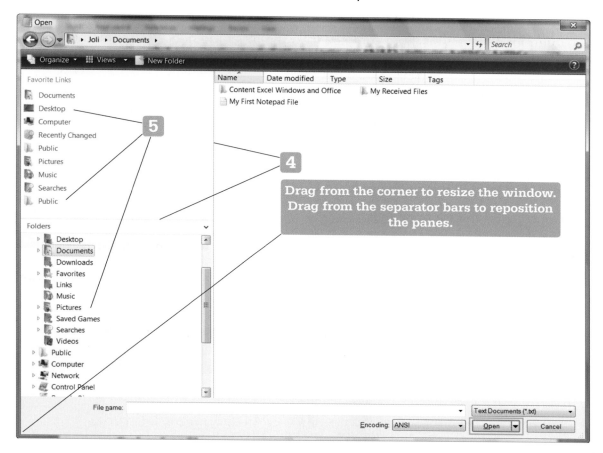

4 Drag from the corner to resize the window. Drag from the separator bars to reposition the panes.

5 In any pane, locate the folder that contains the document to open. Double-click the file to open it.

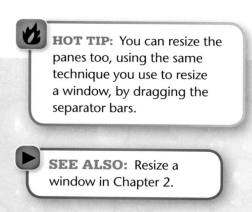

HOT TIP: You can resize the panes too, using the same technique you use to resize a window, by dragging the separator bars.

? DID YOU KNOW?
You can also single-click a file and then click Open.

SEE ALSO: Resize a window in Chapter 2.

Explore for a file

Exploring for a file is a bit more complex than the other methods. In this method, you open Windows Explorer and use the Explorer window to locate the file to open.

1 Right-click the Start button and click Explore.

2 Maximise the window and resize the panes to view the contents of the window.

3 In the left pane, expand and collapse folders until you have located the file to open.

4 Double-click the file to open it.

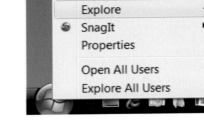

? DID YOU KNOW?
To expand and collapse any folder, click the arrow next to it.

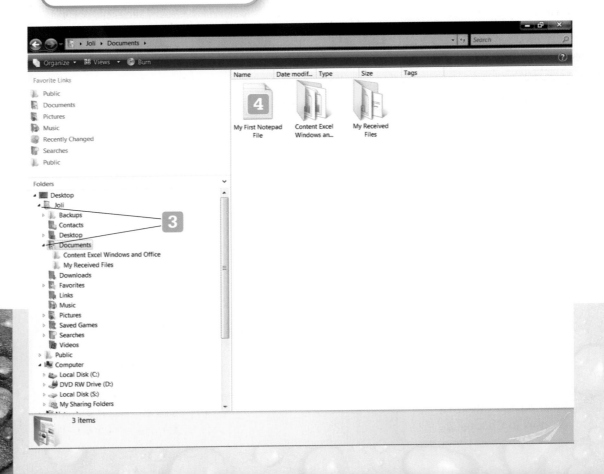

Perform an advanced search

Vista lets you search from the Start Search menu, as you know. Just click Start and in the Start Search dialogue box, type a few letters of what you're looking for and results will appear in a list. If you don't find the results you want though, a more thorough search must be performed. That is easily done by clicking Search Everywhere in the results pane. After clicking Search Everywhere, the results will appear in a new window. Although the results aren't necessarily organised, the results do appear.

1 Click Start.

2 In the Start Search dialogue box, type your own first name.

3 Click Search Everywhere.

4 To sort the results, at the top of the page click Email, Document, Picture, Music or Other.

5 When you've located the file, double-click it to open it.

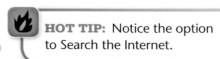

HOT TIP: Notice the option to Search the Internet.

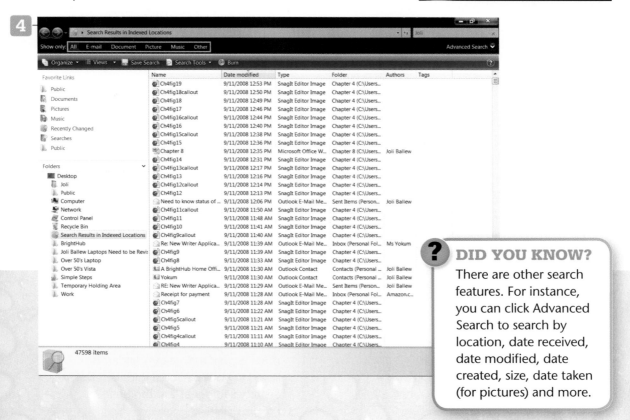

DID YOU KNOW?

There are other search features. For instance, you can click Advanced Search to search by location, date received, date modified, date created, size, date taken (for pictures) and more.

Save search results

Once you perform a search and the search results appear in a window, and even after sorting through the results, you can save the results in a search folder. Once saved, you can access the results any time you like, simply by opening the folder. Search folders are 'smart' too: each time you open the folder after saving it, it performs a new search and adds any new data it finds that matches the search folder's criteria. There are all sorts of uses for search folders, so let your imagination run wild. You can create a search folder for anything you can type into the Start Search dialogue box.

1 Complete the step in Perform an advanced search.

2 Click Save Search.

3 Name the search descriptively.

4 Click Save.

5 Close the Search window by clicking the X in the top right corner.

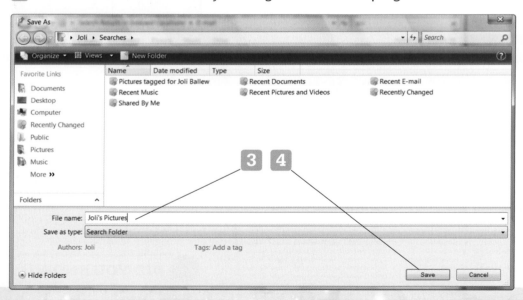

? DID YOU KNOW?

A search folder only offers a place to access data that match the search criteria; it does not move the data there or create copies of data.

🔥 HOT TIP: Once a search folder is saved, you can access it and its contents just like any other folder on your hard drive. By default, search folders are saved in your personal folder, in the Searches folder as a subfolder.

Back up a folder to an external drive

Once you have your data saved in folders, you can copy the folders to an external drive to create a backup. You copy the folder to the external drive in the same way that you would copy a folder to another area of your hard drive: you open both folders and drag and drop.

1 Click Start and click Computer.

2 Locate the external drive. (Leave this window open).

3 Locate a folder to copy.

4 Position the windows so that you can see them both.

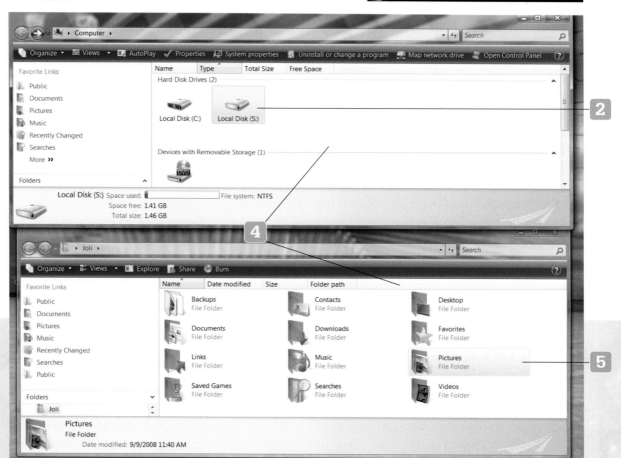

5 Right-click the folder to copy.

6 While holding down the right mouse key, drag the folder to the new location.

7 Drop it there.

8 Choose Copy Here.

 ALERT: Before you begin, plug in and/or attach the external drive.

 HOT TIP: Click Start and click your personal folder (the one with your name on it) to locate a folder to copy.

WHAT DOES THIS MEAN?

Your personal folder contains the following folders, which in turn contain data you've saved:

Contacts: This folder contains your contacts' information, which includes email addresses, pictures, phone numbers, home and business addresses and more.

Desktop: This folder contains links to items for data you've created on your desktop.

Documents: This folder contains documents you've saved, subfolders you've created, and folders created by Vista including Fax, My Received Files, Remote Assistance Logs and Scanned Documents.

Downloads: This folder does not contain anything by default. It does offer a place to save items you download from the Internet, such as drivers and third-party programs.

Favorites: This folder contains the items in Internet Explorer's Favorites list. It may also include folders created by the computer manufacturer or Microsoft, including Links, Microsoft Websites and MSN Websites.

Links: This folder contains shortcuts to the Documents, Music, Pictures, Public, Recently Changed and Searches folders.

Music: This folder contains sample music and music you save to the PC.

Pictures: This folder contains sample pictures and pictures you save to the PC.

Saved Games: This folder contains games that ship with Windows Vista and offers a place to save games you acquire on your own. It may also contain games added by the manufacturer.

Searches: This folder contains preconfigured search folders including Recent Documents, Recent Email, Recent Music, Recent Pictures and Videos, Recently Changed and Shared By Me. If you need to find something recently accessed or changed and don't know where to look, you can probably locate it here. These folders get updated each time you open them.

Videos: This folder contains sample videos and videos you save to the PC.

 SEE ALSO: Restore a window and Move a window in Chapter 2.

 SEE ALSO: Move a folder earlier in this chapter.

ALERT: Don't choose Move Here. This will move the folder off the computer and onto the hard drive.

5 Connecting to and surfing the Internet

Introduction

If you aren't online already, now's the time to take the plunge. There are a few things you'll need to do before you can start surfing the Web and emailing friends and family though, like selecting an Internet service provider (ISP), subscribing to it, selecting a user name, password and email address, and obtaining the required configuration settings. Once you have all of that, you'll be ready to go.

There is one exception to subscribing to an ISP and paying for it monthly: you can visit free or minimal-cost 'hotspots' where you can get online and with no configuration tasks, provided you have a wireless network adapter installed in your PC. If you have a new laptop, you probably do. If you have a desktop PC, you're probably out of luck though. Although you might have a wireless network adapter, you're not going to want to lug your huge PC and a monitor to the local coffee shop just to get online.

Select an ISP

There are a tremendous number of options for connecting to the Internet. You can connect using your phone line (dial-up), using an existing cable connection (broadband or DSL – digital subscriber line) or wirelessly (satellite). You can also use a connection from a mobile phone provider such as T-Mobile, which is often referred to as mobile broadband. This makes choosing an ISP a seemingly daunting task. Making the best choice requires a bit of time and research.

1 Decide where and how you want to access the Internet.

- If you want to connect from anywhere, consider a mobile phone or wireless satellite provider.
- If you want to connect only from home, consider cable, broadband or DSL.
- If you want to connect for free, find a local hotspot (there's more on this later).

2 Decide whether speed matters to you.

- If you don't travel and speed doesn't matter, consider dial-up. It's inexpensive.
- If you don't travel and speed does matter to you, consider DSL or cable.
- If you travel, you have only one option, satellite. It's not lightning fast, but it is faster than dial-up.

3 Decide whether cost plays a large role in your decision.

- If cost is an issue, dial-up is the least expensive.
- If you can afford a medium-sized monthly bill, consider cable, broadband or dial-up.
- If you have the money (and need access from anywhere), consider satellite.
- If you can't afford a monthly subscription, consider free Wi-Fi hotspots at your local library or community centre. You'll need a laptop or the ability to use a public computer.

4 Call companies that offer the service you want. Consider your existing mobile phone, cable or satellite TV provider. Many offer bundled pricing.

? DID YOU KNOW?
Decide on a monthly budget. Go to a friend's house if necessary and visit a web site like www.broadband-finder.co.uk to compare prices and services.

 ALERT: Don't pay a set-up cost. There are too many companies that will set up your connection for free, making this an unnecessary expense. Note that you may have to purchase hardware though.

Check for a wireless network card

If you have a laptop and don't want to pay for Internet service, you can take your laptop to a 'free Internet hotspot' and connect to the Internet at no cost. However, your laptop must have the required wireless hardware. Specifically, you need a built-in wireless card (or a wireless adapter). You can find out whether you have this hardware using Device Manager.

1 Click Start.

2 In the Start Search dialogue box, type Device Manager.

3 Under Programs, click Device Manager to open it.

4 Locate Network Adapters. (Wireless hardware is called network adapters.)

5 Click the plus sign to expand it: it will become a minus sign as shown here.

6 Locate a device with the word 'wireless' in it.

7 If you see a wireless adapter listed, you have the proper hardware for connecting to a hotspot.

8 Click the X in the top right corner of Device Manager to close it.

SEE ALSO: Open an application or program in Chapter 1.

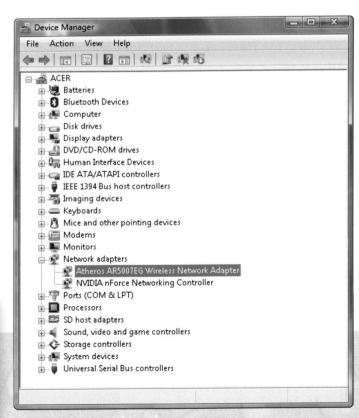

? DID YOU KNOW?

Even if you have no adapters, you can purchase a USB converter to obtain satellite Internet or a modem to use dial-up. There's always a way to get online!

Obtain the proper settings

Once you've decided on an ISP, you'll need to call them to set up the subscription. Although you can set up your new account online, you won't get the personal service you deserve. (And you probably don't have a connection to the Internet anyway!) If, after talking to the representative, you are offered a better deal to subscribe online, consider trekking to a friend's house to do it. However, if you explain you don't have access, you may get the better deal anyway. It doesn't hurt to ask.

There are some important things to ask the representative and you must write these things down and keep them in a safe place:

1 User name.

2 Email address.

3 Password.

4 Incoming POP3 server name.

5 Outgoing SMTP server name.

6 Account name (may be the same as user name).

 HOT TIP: Ask whether the company will be mailing you a cable modem, wireless card or wireless modem, or other device. Also, ask if there's an extra fee for having someone to your home to set it up.

ALERT: You'll need this information to set up your email account and to log on to the Internet using your paid service.

Create a connection

Before you can connect to the Internet, you need to install any hardware you have received. This may mean connecting a cable modem, wireless access point or DSL modem. If you get in a bind, call the ISP. They are there to help; it's their job. Once the hardware is set up, and if the ISP does not walk you through the process of configuring the connection in Windows Vista, you'll need to access the Network and Sharing Center to create the connection yourself.

1 Click Start.

2 In the Start Search window, type Network and Sharing.

3 Under Programs, select Network and Sharing Center.

4 Under Tasks, click Set up a connection or network.

5 Click Connect to the Internet – Set up a wireless, broadband, or dial-up connection to the Internet. Click Next.

> **SEE ALSO:** Open an application or program in Chapter 1.

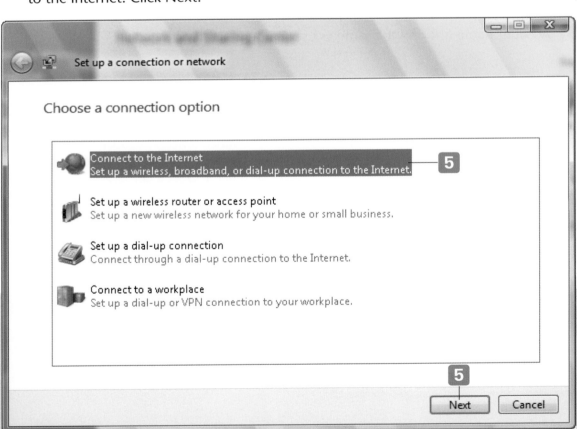

6 Select either broadband or dial-up, based on the ISP's connection option, and click Next.

7 For broadband:

- Type your user name and password.
- Select Remember this password (otherwise you'll have to type the password each time you use the connection).
- If desired, type a new connection name.
- If you have a home network and want to share this computer with others on the network, tick Allow other people to use this connection.
- Click Connect.

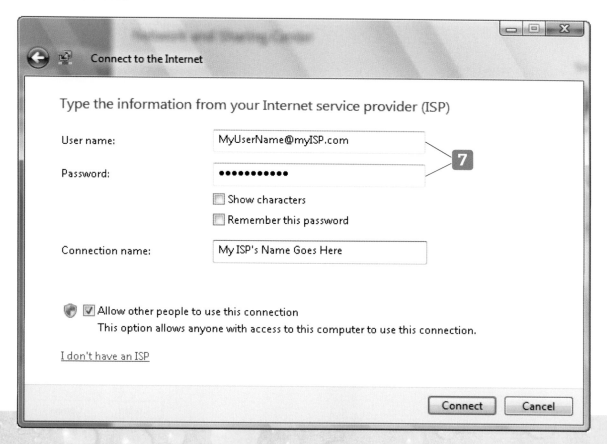

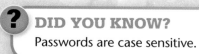
DID YOU KNOW?
Passwords are case sensitive.

8 For dial-up:

- Type the phone number.
- Click Dialing Rules. Input the proper information and click OK.
- Type your user name and password.
- Select Remember this password (otherwise you'll have to type the password each time you use the connection).
- If desired, type a new connection name.
- If you have a home network and want to share this computer with others on the network, tick Allow other people to use this connection.
- Click Create.

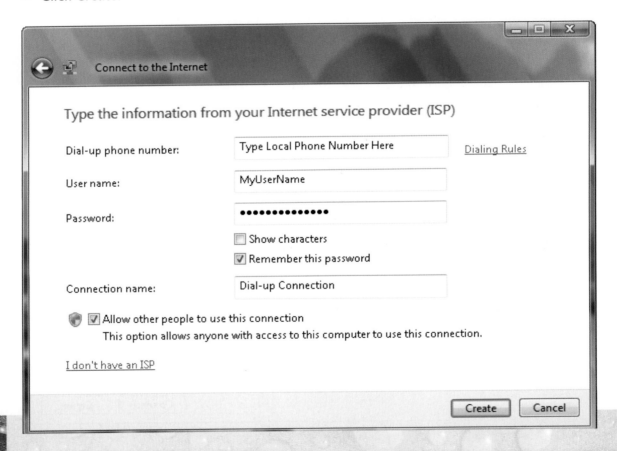

ALERT: The phone number should be a local number, otherwise you'll incur dial-up charges.

Enable Network Discovery

Network Discovery tells Vista that you're interested in seeing, and possibly joining, other networks. You may want to connect a new Vista computer to an existing network in your home. If you have a laptop, you may want to connect to a public network in your local coffee shop. You will have to enable Network Discovery to be able to view and ultimately join available networks.

1 Click Start.

2 In the Start Search window, type Network and Sharing Center. Click Network and Sharing Center.

3 Under Sharing and Discovery, click the down arrow next to Off by Network discovery. It will become an upwards arrow.

4 Click Turn on network discovery unless it is already turned on.

5 Click Apply.

6 Click the X to close the Network and Sharing Center.

? DID YOU KNOW?

The Network and Sharing Center is also where you set up file sharing, public folder sharing, printer sharing, password-protected sharing, and media sharing.

? DID YOU KNOW?

You can click in the Tasks pane to view computers and devices on your home network and manage network connections.

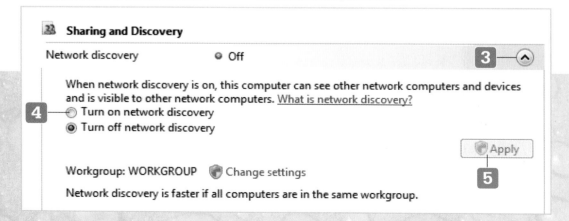

Diagnose connection problems

If you are having trouble connecting to the Internet through a public or private network, you can diagnose Internet problems using the Network and Sharing Center.

1 Open the Network and Sharing Center.

2 To diagnose a non-working Internet connection, click Diagnose and repair.

3 Click the first solution to resolve the connectivity problem.

4 Often, the problem is resolved. If it is not, move to the next step and the next until it is.

5 Click the X in the top right corner of the Network and Sharing Centre window to close it.

SEE ALSO: Enable Network Discovery in the previous section.

ALERT: If you are connected to the Internet, you will see a green line between your computer and the Internet. If you are not connected, you will see a red X.

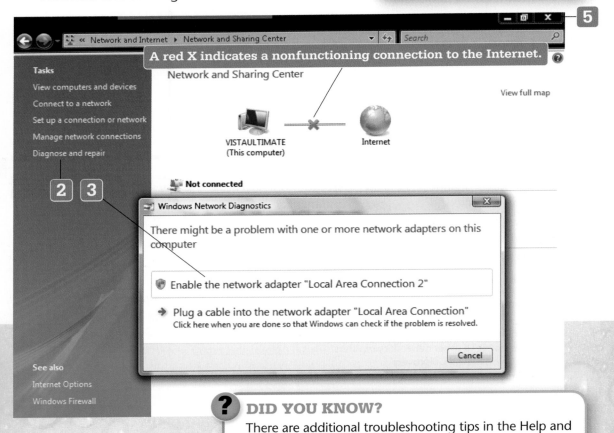

A red X indicates a nonfunctioning connection to the Internet.

Tasks
View computers and devices
Connect to a network
Set up a connection or network
Manage network connections
Diagnose and repair

See also
Internet Options
Windows Firewall

Network and Sharing Center

View full map

VISTAULTIMATE
(This computer)

Internet

Not connected

Windows Network Diagnostics

There might be a problem with one or more network adapters on this computer

Enable the network adapter "Local Area Connection 2"

→ Plug a cable into the network adapter "Local Area Connection"
Click here when you are done so that Windows can check if the problem is resolved.

Cancel

? DID YOU KNOW?
There are additional troubleshooting tips in the Help and Support pages. Click Start, then click Help and Support.

Join a network

When you connect a new PC running Windows Vista to a wired network or get within range of a wireless one (and you have wireless hardware installed in your computer), Vista will find the network and then ask you what kind of network it is. It's a public network if you're in a coffee shop, library or café, and it's a private network if it's a network you manage, like one already in your home.

1 Connect physically to a wired network using an Ethernet cable or, if you have wireless hardware installed in your laptop, get within range of a wireless network.

2 Select Home, Work or Public location. (If necessary input credentials.)

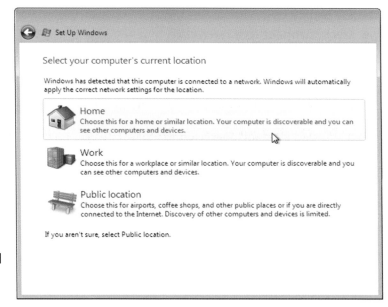

3 Look for either of these icons in the bottom right corner of your screen. It means you are connected to the Internet and/or a local network.

 HOT TIP: When a network is accessible, either because you've connected to it using an Ethernet cable or through a wireless network card inside your PC, the Set Network Location wizard will appear.

? DID YOU KNOW?

Connecting to an existing network allows you to access shared features of the network. In a coffee shop that's likely only to be a connection to the Internet; if it's a home network, it's your personal, shared data (and probably a connection to the Internet too).

 DID YOU KNOW?

An icon with an X through it means you are not connected.

Connect to a free hotspot

Wi-Fi hot spots are popping up all over the country in coffee shops, parks, libraries, all sorts of places. Wi-Fi hotspots let you connect to the Internet without having to be tethered to an Ethernet cable or tied down with a high monthly wireless bill. You may also have to buy a cup of coffee for the privilege, but hey, you were going to anyway, right?

1 Turn on your wireless laptop within range of a free hot spot.

2 Click Connect to a network.

3 Click Connect.

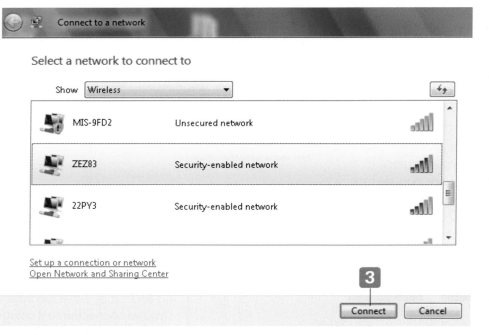

Open a website in Internet Explorer

Internet Explorer comes with Windows Vista and is an application you use to surf the Internet. Internet Explorer is a 'web browser' and it has everything you need, including a pop-up blocker, zoom settings and the ability to save your favourite webpages. You'll use Internet Explorer to surf the Internet.

1 Open Internet Explorer. A website will probably open automatically.

2 To open a new website, drag your mouse across the website name to select it. Do not drag your mouse over the http://www part of the address.

3 Type the name of the website you'd like to visit in the address bar. Try http://www.amazon.com.

4 Press Enter on the keyboard.

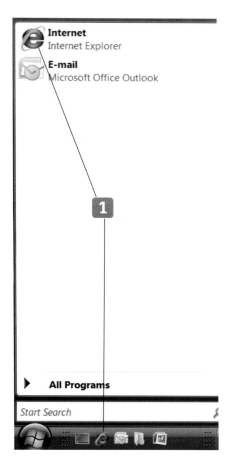

SEE ALSO: Open an application or program in Chapter 1.

HOT TIP: You can open Internet Explorer a number of ways; just look for the blue e.

ALERT: Web sites almost always start with http://www.

? **DID YOU KNOW?**

.com is the most popular website ending and it means the website is a company, business or personal site. .edu is used for educational institutions, .gov for government entities, .org for non-profit organisations (mostly) and .net for miscellaneous businesses and companies or personal websites. There are others though, including .info, .biz, .tv and .uk.com.

Open a website in a new tab

You can open more than one website at a time in Internet Explorer. To do this, click the tab that appears to the right of the open webpage. Then, type the name of the website you'd like to visit.

1 Open Internet Explorer.

2 Click an empty tab.

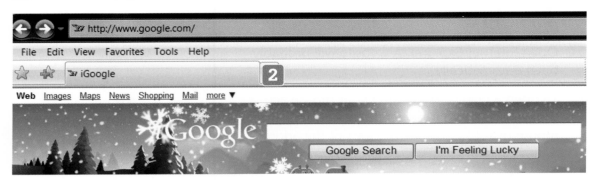

3 Type the name of the website you'd like to visit in the address bar.

4 Press Enter on the keyboard.

HOT TIP: Type the following:
http://www.microsoft.com/uk

DID YOU KNOW?

When a web site name starts with https://, it means it's secure. When purchasing items online, make sure the payment pages have this prefix.

Set a home page

You can select a single webpage or multiple webpages to be displayed each time you open Internet Explorer. In fact, there are three options for configuring home pages:

- **Use this webpage as your only home page:** select this option if you want only one page to serve as your home page.
- **Add this webpage to your home pages tabs:** select this option if you want this page to be one of several home pages.
- **Use the current tab set as your home page:** select this option if you've opened multiple tabs and you want all of them to be home pages.

1 Use the Address bar to locate a webpage you want to use as your home page.

2 Click the arrow next to the Home icon.

3 Click Add or Change Home Page.

4 Make a selection using the information provided regarding each option.

5 Click Yes.

6 Repeat these steps as desired.

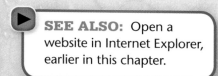

SEE ALSO: Open a website in Internet Explorer, earlier in this chapter.

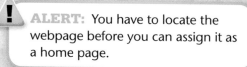

ALERT: You have to locate the webpage before you can assign it as a home page.

Mark a favourite

Favourites are websites you save links to for accessing more easily at a later time. They differ from home pages because by default they do not open when you start Internet Explorer. The favourites you save appear in the Favorites Center, which you can access by clicking the large yellow star on the Command bar. You will see some favourites listed, including Microsoft Websites and MSN Websites. Every time you save a favourite, it will appear here.

1 Go to the webpage you want to configure as a favourite.

2 Click the Add to Favorites icon.

3 To add a single webpage as a favourite, click Add to Favourites.

4 Type a name for the website when prompted.

5 Click Add.

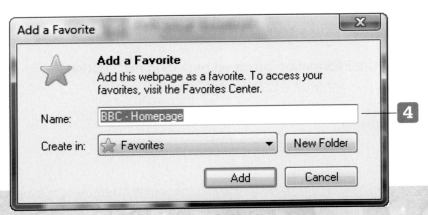

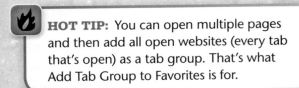
HOT TIP: You can open multiple pages and then add all open websites (every tab that's open) as a tab group. That's what Add Tab Group to Favorites is for.

HOT TIP: You can organise your favourites in your personal Favorites folder.

Change the zoom level of a webpage

If you have trouble reading what's on a webpage because the text is too small, use the Page Zoom feature. Page Zoom works by preserving the fundamental design of the webpage you're viewing. This means that Page Zoom intelligently zooms in on the entire page, which maintains the page's integrity, layout and look.

1 Open Internet Explorer and browse to a webpage.

2 Click the arrow located at the bottom right of Internet Explorer to show the Zoom options.

3 Click 150%.

4 Notice how the webpage text and images increase. Use the scroll bars to navigate the page.

? DID YOU KNOW?

The term 'browse' is used both to describe locating a file on your hard drive and locating something on the Internet.

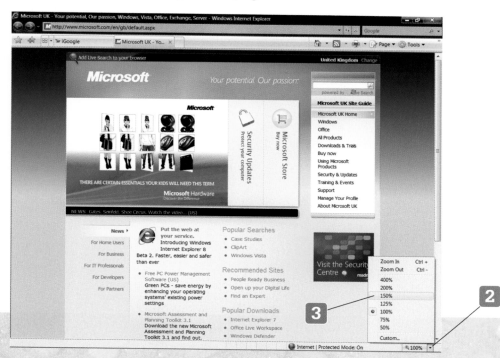

? DID YOU KNOW?

The Page Zoom options are located under the Page icon on the Command Bar, under Zoom, but it's much easier to use the link at the bottom right of the browser window, on the Status bar.

Print a webpage

To print a webpage, simply click the Print icon on the Command bar.

1 Open Internet Explorer and browse to a webpage.

2 Click the Print icon on the command bar.

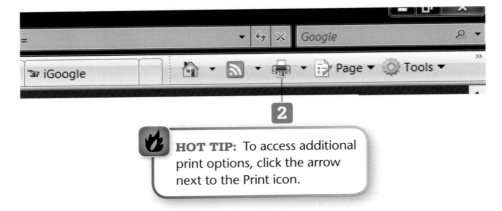

2

HOT TIP: To access additional print options, click the arrow next to the Print icon.

Clear history

If you don't want people to be able to snoop around on your computer and find out what sites you've been visiting you'll need to delete your browsing history. Deleting your browsing history lets you remove the information stored on your computer related to your Internet activities.

1 Open Internet Explorer.

2 Click the Alt key on the keyboard.

3 Click Tools.

4 Click Delete Browsing History.

5 To delete any or all of the listed items, click the Delete button.

6 Click Close when finished.

ALERT: Clicking the Alt key on the keyboard is what causes the Menu bar to appear.

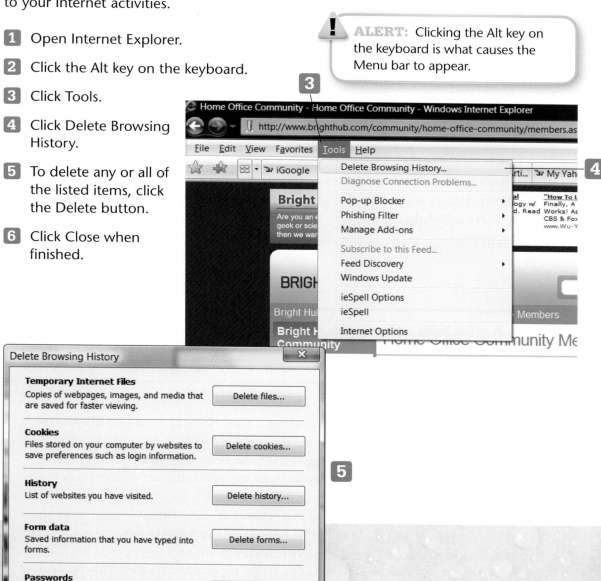

Stay safe online

There's a chapter in this book on security, Chapter 7. In it, you'll learn how to use Windows Firewall, Windows Defender and other Security Center features. However, much of staying secure when online and surfing the Internet has more to do with common sense. When you're online, make sure you follow the guidelines listed here.

- If you are connecting to a public network, make sure you select Public when prompted by Windows Vista.
- Always keep your PC secure with anti-virus software.
- Limit the amount of confidential information you store on the Internet.
- When making credit card purchases or travel reservations, always make sure the website address starts with https://.
- Always sign out of any secure website you enter.

 DID YOU KNOW?
When you connect to a network you know, like a network in your home, you select Home (or Work).

 ALERT: You have to purchase and install your own antivirus software; it does not come with Vista.

 ALERT: Don't put your address and phone number on Facebook or other social networking sites.

Joli Ballew | **Edit Profile** | Writer Dashboard | Sign out

 HOT TIP: The 's' after http lets you know it's a secure site.

WHAT DOES THIS MEAN?

There are three network options and when you see the Set Network Location dialogue box, you need to select one. Here's how to know which one to choose:

- **Home:** Choose this if the network is your home network or a network you trust (such as a network at a friend's house). This connection type lets your computer *discover* other PCs, printers and devices on the network and they can see you.
- **Work:** Choose this if you are connecting to a network at work. The settings for Work and Home are the same, only the titles differ so you can tell them apart easily.
- **Public location:** Choose this if the network you want to connect to is open to anyone within range of it, such as networks in coffee shops, airports and libraries. Vista figures that if you choose Public, you only want to connect to the Internet and nothing else. It closes down *discoverability*, so that even your shared data are safe.

Address bar: Used to type in Internet addresses, also known as URLs (uniform resource locators). Generally, an Internet address takes the form of http://www.*companyname*.com.

The Internet Explorer interface has several distinct parts:

- **Command bar:** Used to access icons such as the Home and Print icons.
- **Tabs:** Used to access websites when multiple sites are open.
- **Search Window:** Used to search for anything on the Internet.

Temporary Internet files: These are files that have been downloaded and saved in your Temporary Internet Files folder. A snooper could go through these files to see what you've been doing online.

Cookies: These are small text files that include data that identify your preferences when you visit particular websites. Cookies are what allow you to visit, say, www.amazon.com and be greeted with Hello <your name>, We have recommendations for you! Cookies help a site offer you a personalised web experience.

History: This is the list of websites you've visited and any web addresses you've typed. Anyone can look at your History list to see where you've been.

Passwords: These are passwords that were saved using Internet Explorer autocomplete password prompts.

Domain Name: For our use here, a domain name is synonymous with a website name.

Favourite: A webpage that you've chosen to maintain a shortcut for in the Favorites Center.

Home page: The webpage that opens when you open IE7. You can set the home page and configure additional pages to open as well.

Link: A shortcut to a webpage. Links are often offered in an email, document or webpage to allow you to access a site without having to actually type in its name. In almost all instances, links are underlined and in a different colour than the page they are configured on.

Navigate: The process of moving from one webpage to another or viewing items on a single webpage. Often the term is used as follows: 'Click the link to navigate to the new webpage.'

Search: A term used when you type a word or group of words into a Search window. Searching for data produces results.

Scroll up and scroll down: A process of using the scroll bars on a webpage or the arrow keys on a keyboard to move up and down the pages of a website.

Website: A group of webpages that contain related information. Microsoft's website contains information about Microsoft products, for instance.

URL: The information you type to access a website, such as http://www.microsoft.com.

6 Working with email

Introduction

Windows Mail is included in all editions of Microsoft Windows Vista and is the only thing you need to view, send and receive email, manage your contacts and manage sent, saved and incoming email. Within Windows Mail you can also print email, create folders for storing email you want to keep, manage unwanted email, open attachments, send pictures inside an email and more.

To use Windows Mail, you need an email address and two email server addresses, all of which you can get from your ISP. In fact, you probably have this information if you worked through Chapter 5, Connecting to and surfing the Internet. With this information in hand, you'll work through the New Connection Wizard, inputting the required information when prompted, to set up the program. Once Mail is set up, you're ready to send and receive mail. Don't worry, it's easy!

Set up an email account in Windows Mail

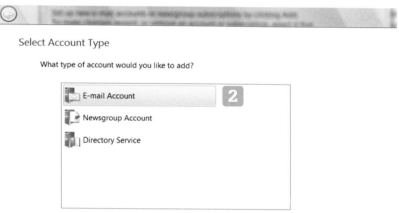

The first time you open Windows Mail you'll be prompted to input the required information regarding your email address and email servers. That's because Windows Mail is a program for sending and receiving email and you can't do that without inputting the proper information.

1 Click Start, then click Windows Mail.

2 Click Email Account. Click Next.

Select Account Type

What type of account would you like to add?

> E-mail Account **2**
> Newsgroup Account
> Directory Service

What information do I need to set up my account?

Next   Cancel

2

3 Type your display name. Click Next.

4 Type your email address. Click next.

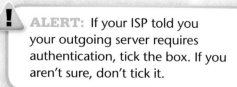

ALERT: If your ISP told you your outgoing server requires authentication, tick the box. If you aren't sure, don't tick it.

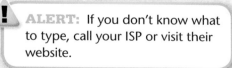

ALERT: If you don't know what to type, call your ISP or visit their website.

Set up e-mail servers

Incoming e-mail server type:

POP3 ▼

Incoming mail (POP3 or IMAP) server:

Outgoing e-mail server (SMTP) name:

☐ Outgoing server requires authentication

Where can I find my e-mail server information?

Next   Cancel

5

5 Fill in the information for your incoming and outgoing mail servers. Click Next.

6 Type your email user name and password. Click Next.

7 Click Finish.

 HOT TIP: Leave Remember Password ticked and Mail will remember it.

 ALERT: To resolve errors, in the Internet Accounts dialogue box, which will still be available, click the email address to repair, and click Properties.

View an email

Windows Mail checks for email automatically when you first open the program and every 30 minutes thereafter. If you want to check for email manually, you can click the Send/Receive button at any time. When you receive mail, there are two ways to read it. You can click the message once and read it in the Mail window or double-click it to open it in its own window. I think it's best to simply click the email once, that way you don't have multiple open windows to deal with.

1 Click the Send/Receive button.

2 Click the email once.

3 View the contents of the email.

! ALERT: Email is received in the Inbox. If Inbox is not selected, you must select it first!

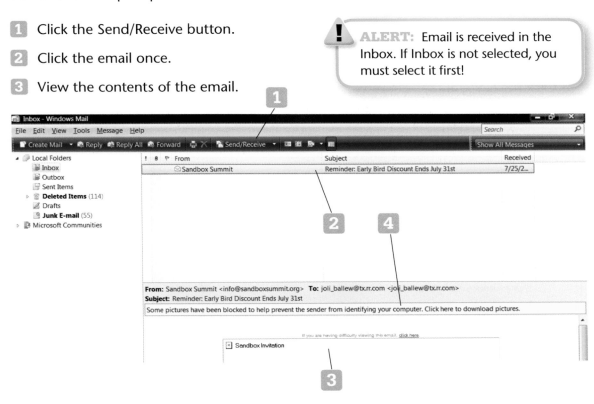

4 If you can't see the pictures in the email, click the yellow bar.

! ALERT: Click to view pictures only if you know the sender. If you view the pictures in a spam message, the spammer will know your email address works (and send you more spam).

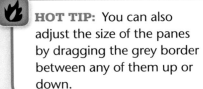

🔥 HOT TIP: You can also adjust the size of the panes by dragging the grey border between any of them up or down.

Change how often Mail checks for email

You may want to configure Mail to check for email more or less often than every 30 minutes. It's easy to make the change.

1 Click Tools.

2 Click Options.

3 Click the General tab.

4 Change the number of minutes from 30 to something else.

5 Click OK.

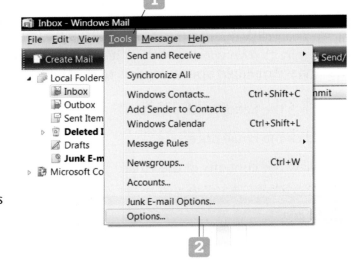

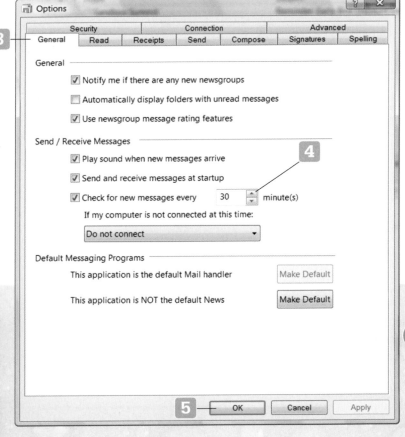

? DID YOU KNOW?

You can change other settings in Mail from the other tabs in the Options dialogue box.

View an attachment

An attachment is a file that you can send with an email, such as a picture, document, video clip or something similar. If an email you receive contains an attachment, you'll see a paperclip. To open the attachment, click the paperclip icon in the Preview pane and click the attachment's name.

1 Click the email once in the Message pane.

2 Click the paperclip in the Preview pane.

3 Click the name of the attachment.

4 Click Open.

! ALERT: Hackers send attachments that look like they are from legitimate companies, banks and online services. Do not open these unless you are absolutely positive they're from a company you trust.

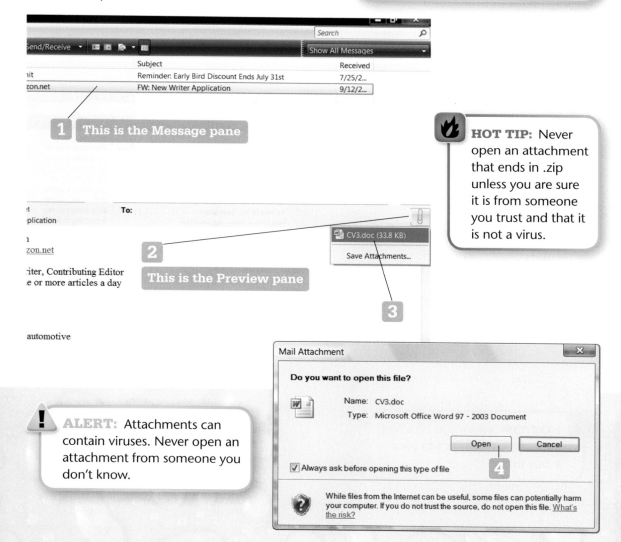

HOT TIP: Never open an attachment that ends in .zip unless you are sure it is from someone you trust and that it is not a virus.

! ALERT: Attachments can contain viruses. Never open an attachment from someone you don't know.

Recover email from the Junk E-mail folder

Windows Mail has a junk email filter where anything considered spam gets sent. Unfortunately, sometimes emails get sent to the Junk Email folder that are actually legitimate. Therefore, once a week or so you should look in this folder to see whether any emails you want to keep are in there.

1 Click the Junk E-mail folder once.

2 Use the scroll bar if necessary to browse through the email in the folder.

3 If you see an email that is legitimate, click it once.

4 Click Not Junk.

HOT TIP: When you tell Mail that a certain email is 'not junk', it remembers and should not flag email from this sender as spam again.

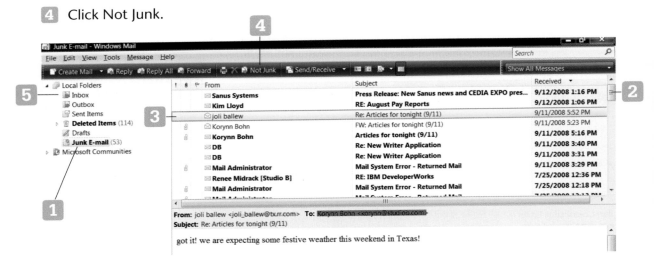

5 After reviewing the files, click Inbox.

HOT TIP: When you click Not Junk, the email is sent to your Inbox folder.

ALERT: Mail requires routine maintenance including deleting email from the Junk E-mail folder, among others. You'll learn how to delete items in a folder later in this chapter.

Reply to an email

When someone sends you an email, you may need to send a reply back to them. You do that by selecting the email and then clicking the Reply button.

1 Select the email you want to reply to in the Message pane.

2 Click Reply.

3 In the To: field, type the email address for the recipient.

4 Type a subject in the Subject field.

5 Type the message in the body pane.

6 Click Send.

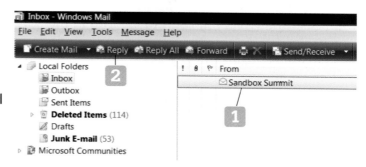

HOT TIP: To send a single email to multiple recipients, separate each email address with a semicolon.

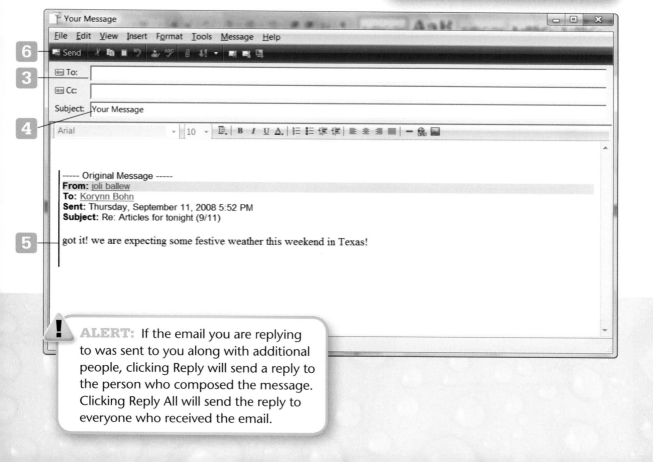

ALERT: If the email you are replying to was sent to you along with additional people, clicking Reply will send a reply to the person who composed the message. Clicking Reply All will send the reply to everyone who received the email.

Forward an email

When someone sends you an email that you want to share with others, you forward the email. You do that by selecting the email and then clicking the Forward button.

1 Select the email you want to forward in the Message pane.

2 Click Forward.

2

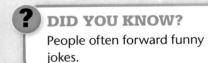

3 In the To: field, type the email address for the recipient.

4 Type a subject in the Subject field.

5 Type the message in the body pane.

6 Click Send.

 HOT TIP: Mail offers formatting tools that you can use to change the font, font colour, font size and more.

? **DID YOU KNOW?**
People often forward funny jokes.

? **DID YOU KNOW?**
Forwarded email contains FW: in the subject line by default.

Compose and send a new email

You compose an email message by clicking Create Mail on the toolbar. You input who the email should be sent to, the subject and then you type the message.

1 Click Create Mail.

2 Type the recipient's email address in the To: line. If you want to add additional names, separate each email address by a semicolon.

3 Type a subject in the Subject field.

4 Type the message in the body pane.

5 Click Send.

 DID YOU KNOW?

In Mail there's a menu bar and a toolbar, which you can use to access other features including tools you're already familiar with like Cut, Copy and Paste, spell check, font, font size, font colour and font style, among other things.

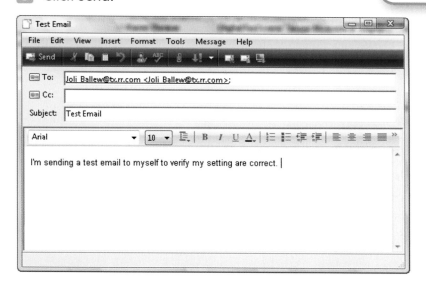

 DID YOU KNOW?

If you want to send the email to someone and you don't need them to respond, you can put them in the CC line.

DID YOU KNOW?

If you want to send the email to someone and you don't want other recipients to know you included them in the email, add them to the Bcc line. (You can show this line by clicking View and then clicking All Headers.)

DID YOU KNOW?

You can choose Tools and click Select Recipients to choose multiple recipients from your Contact list. This way you can add multiple recipients quickly.

Attach a picture to an email using Insert

Although an email that contains only text serves its purpose quite a bit of the time, often you'll want to send a photograph, short video, sound recording, document or other data. When you want to add something to your message other than text, it's called adding an attachment. There are many ways to attach something to an email. One way is to use the Insert menu and choose File Attachment. Then, you can browse to the location of the attachment and click Insert.

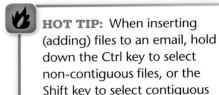

HOT TIP: When inserting (adding) files to an email, hold down the Ctrl key to select non-contiguous files, or the Shift key to select contiguous ones.

1 Click Create Mail.

2 Click Insert.

3 Click File Attachment.

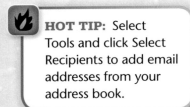

HOT TIP: Select Tools and click Select Recipients to add email addresses from your address book.

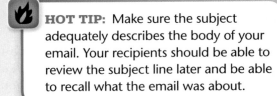

HOT TIP: Make sure the subject adequately describes the body of your email. Your recipients should be able to review the subject line later and be able to recall what the email was about.

4 If the item you want to attach is saved in your Documents folder, skip to step 6.

5 If the item you want to attach is not in the Documents folder, browse to the location of the folder.

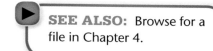

SEE ALSO: Browse for a file in Chapter 4.

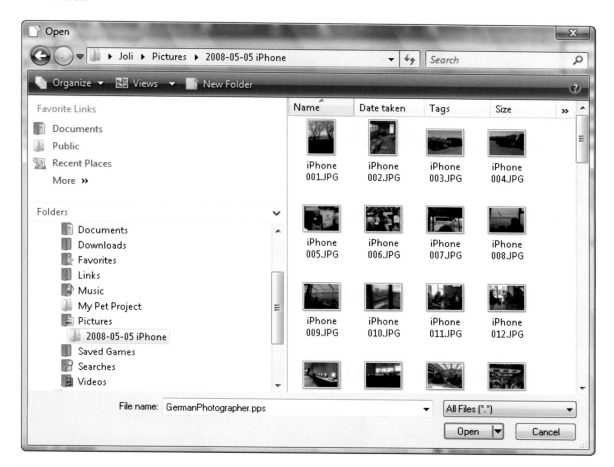

6 Click the item to add and select Open.

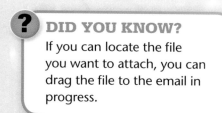
DID YOU KNOW?
If you can locate the file you want to attach, you can drag the file to the email in progress.

ALERT: Anything you attach won't be removed from your computer; instead, a copy will be created for the attachment.

Attach a picture to an email using right-click

You can create an email that contains an attachment by right-clicking the file you want to attach. This method attaches the files to a new email, which is fine if you want to create a new email. The only problem with this is that it doesn't work if you'd rather send forwards or replies. However, this method has a feature other methods don't. With this method, you can resize any images you've selected before sending them. This is a great perk because many pictures are too large to send via email and resizing them helps manage an email's size.

1 Locate the file you'd like to attach and right-click it.

2 Point to Send To.

3 Click Mail Recipient.

4 If the item you're attaching is a picture, choose the picture size.

> **? DID YOU KNOW?**
> You can email from within applications, such as Microsoft Word or Excel. Generally, you'll find the desired option under the File menu, as a submenu of Send.

> **! ALERT:** Avoid sending large attachments, especially to people you know have a dial-up modem or those who get email only on a small device like a BlackBerry, iPhone or Mobile PC.

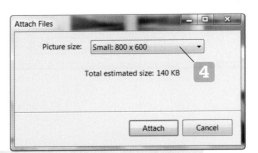

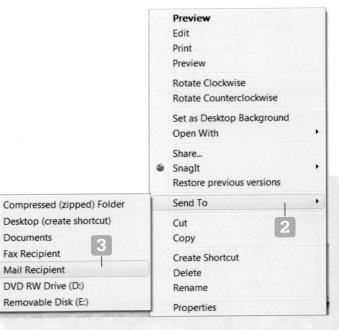

> **? DID YOU KNOW?**
> 800 × 600 is usually the best option when sending pictures via email.

Add a contact

A contact is a data file that holds the information you keep about a person. The contact information looks like a contact card and the information can include a picture, email address, mailing address, first and last name and similar data. By default, Windows Mail creates a contact for each person you email and the data includes the email address. You don't need to do anything to the contacts Windows Mail creates unless you want to add data to a contact.

? DID YOU KNOW?

When someone gives you their email address and other personal data, you can create a contact card for them. From the File menu, select New, then select Contact.

1 From Windows Mail, click the Contacts icon on the toolbar.

2 Click New Contact.

3 Type all of the information you desire to add. Be sure to add information to each tab.

Contacts

4 Click OK.

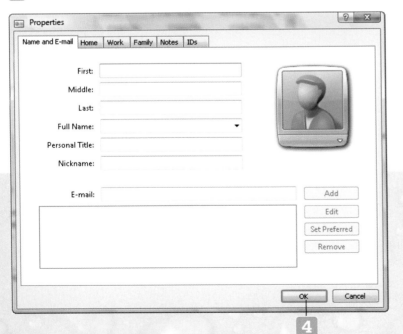

🔥 HOT TIP: Your contacts are stored in your Contacts folder inside your personal folder.

Print an email

Sometimes you'll need to print an email or its attachment. Windows Mail makes it easy to print. Just click the printer icon on the toolbar. After clicking the Print icon, the Print dialogue box will appear where you can select a printer, set print preferences, choose a page range and, well, print.

1 Select the email to print by clicking it in the Message pane.

2 Click the Print icon.

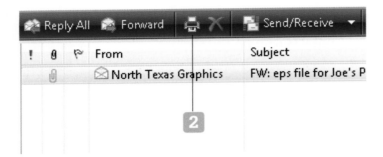

3 In the Print dialogue box, select the printer to use, if more than one exists.

4 Click Print.

Note: You can configure print preferences and choose what pages to print using Preferences. Refer to your printer's user manual to find out what print options your printer supports.

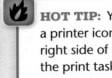 **HOT TIP:** You should see a printer icon appear on the right side of the taskbar during the print task. Click it for more information.

Apply a junk email filter

Just like you receive unwanted information from telesales people, radio stations and television ads, you're going to get unwanted advertisements in emails. This is referred to as junk email or spam. Most of these advertisements are scams and rip-offs, and they also often contain pornographic images. There are four filtering options in Windows Mail: No Automatic Filtering, Low, High and Safe List Only.

1 Click Tools.

2 Click Junk Email Options.

3 From the Options tab, make a selection. We suggest starting at Low and moving to High if necessary later.

4 Click the Phishing tab.

5 Select Protect my Inbox from messages with potential Phishing links. Additionally, move phishing email to the Junk Email folder.

6 Click OK.

ALERT: Never buy anything from a junk email, send money to a sick or dying person you don't know or for your portion of a lottery ticket or fall for other spam hoaxes.

ALERT: Don't give your email address to any website or company or include it in any registration card, unless you're willing to receive junk email from them and their constituents.

ALERT: Check the junk email folder often to make sure no legitimate email has been moved there.

SEE ALSO: Recover email from the Junk E-mail folder, earlier in this chapter.

Create a folder

It's important to perform some housekeeping chores once a month or so. If you don't, Windows Mail may get bogged down and perform more slowly than it should, or you may be unable to manage the email you want to keep. One way you can keep Mail under control is to create a new folder to hold email you want to keep and move mail into it.

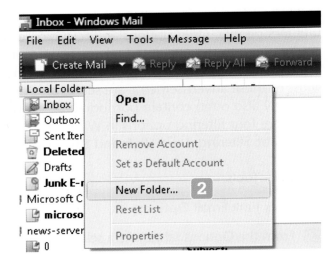

1 Right-click Local Folders.

2 Select New Folder.

3 Type a name for the new folder.

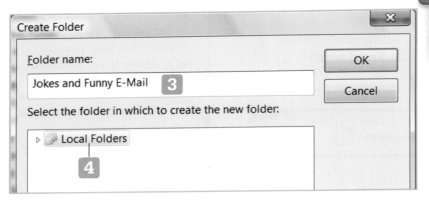

HOT TIP: Name folders descriptively, such as Funny Jokes, Receipts or Pictures.

4 Select Local Folders.

5 Click OK.

6 Note the new folder in the Local Folders list.

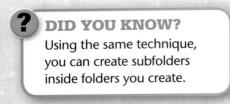

DID YOU KNOW?
Using the same technique, you can create subfolders inside folders you create.

Move email to a folder

Moving an email from one folder (like your Inbox) to another (like Funny Jokes) is a simple task. Just drag the email from one folder to the other.

1 Right-click the email message to move in the Message pane.

2 Hold the mouse button down while dragging the message to the new folder.

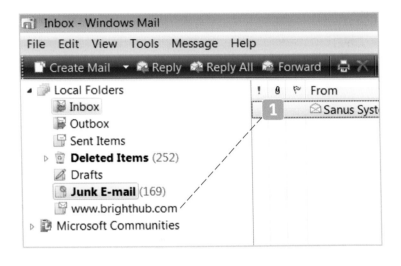

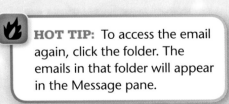 **HOT TIP:** To access the email again, click the folder. The emails in that folder will appear in the Message pane.

Delete email in a folder

In order to keep Mail from getting bogged down, you'll need to delete email in folders regularly. Depending on how much email you get, this may be as often as once a week.

1 Right-click Junk E-mail.

2 Click Empty 'Junk E-mail' Folder.

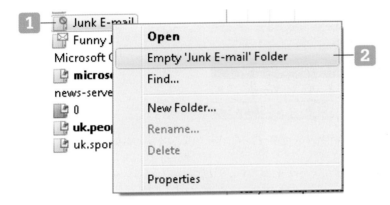

3 Right-click Deleted Items.

4 Click Empty 'Deleted Items' Folder.

 **HOT TIP:** Select any email in any folder and click the red X to delete it.

WHAT DOES THIS MEAN?

Display name: This is the name that will appear in the From field when you compose an email, and in the sender's Inbox (under From in their email list) when people receive email from you. Don't put your email address here; put your first and last name and any additional information.

Email address: The email address you chose when you signed up with your ISP. It often takes this form: *yourname@yourispname.com.*

Mail servers: The name of the computer that handles your incoming and outgoing email.

Email user name and password: Often your user name is your email address. Passwords are a security measure and are case sensitive.

Spam: Junk email, unwanted email, sales ads.

Inbox: This folder holds mail you've received.

Outbox: This folder holds mail you've written but have not yet sent.

Sent Items: This folder stores copies of messages you've sent.

Deleted Items: This folder holds mail you've deleted.

Drafts: This folder holds messages you've started and saved, but not completed. Click File and click Save to put an email in progress here.

Junk Email: This folder holds email that Windows Mail thinks is spam. You should check this folder occasionally, since Mail may put email in there you want to read.

Microsoft Communities: This folder offers access to available Microsoft Newsgroups and communities.

CC: Stands for carbon copy.

Bcc: Stands for blind carbon copy and is a secret copy.

No Automatic Filtering: Use this only if you do not want Windows Mail to block junk email messages. Windows Mail will continue to block messages from email addresses listed on the Blocked Senders list.

Low: Use this option if you receive very little junk email. You can start here and increase the filter if it becomes necessary.

High: Use this option if you receive a lot of junk email and want to block as much of it as possible. Use this option for children's email accounts. Note that some valid emails will probably be blocked, so you'll have to review the Junk Email folder occasionally to make sure you aren't missing any you want to keep.

Safe List Only: Use this option if you only want to receive messages from people or domain names on your Safe Senders list. This is a drastic step and requires you to add every sender you want to receive mail from to the Safe Senders list. Use this as a last resort.

Phishing: This is the act of trying to acquire sensitive information such as user names, passwords and credit card information. Phishing emails try to get you to respond with personal information, while websites try to obtain that information by tricking you into believing that you are visiting a legitimate website and getting you to input information manually.

7 Stay secure

Introduction

Windows Vista comes with a lot of built-in features to keep you and your data safe. Vista security tools and features help you avoid email scams, harmful websites and hackers, and also help you protect your data and your computer from unscrupulous co-workers or nosy family members. If you know how to take advantage of the available safeguards, you'll be protected in almost all cases. You just need to be aware of the dangers, heed security warnings when they are given (and resolve them) and use all of the available features in Vista to protect yourself and your PC.

Add a new user account

You created your user account when you first turned on your new Vista PC. Your user account is what defines your personal folders as well as your settings for desktop background, screen saver and other items. You are the 'administrator' of your computer. If you share the PC with someone, they should have their own user account too.

ALERT: If every person who accesses your PC has their own standard user account and password, and if every person logs on using that account and then logs off the PC each time they've finished using it, you'll never have to worry about anyone accessing anyone else's personal data.

1 Click Start.

2 Click Control Panel.

3 Click Add or remove user accounts.

- **Control Panel Home**
  Classic View

System and Maintenance
Get started with Windows
Back up your computer

Security
Check for updates
Check this computer's security status
Allow a program through Windows Firewall

Network and Internet
View network status and tasks
Set up file sharing

Hardware and Sound
Play CDs or other media automatically
Printer
Mouse

Programs
Uninstall a program
Change startup programs

User Accounts and Family Safety
Set up parental controls for any user
Add or remove user accounts

Appearance and Personalization
Change desktop background
Customize colors
Adjust screen resolution

Clock, Language, and Region
Change keyboards or other input methods

Ease of Access
Let Windows suggest settings
Optimize visual display

Additional Options

Recent Tasks
Add or remove user accounts — **3**
Uninstall a program
Change your Windows password

4 Click Create a new account.

5 Type a new account name.

6 Verify Standard user is selected.

7 Click Create account.

Note: You can also click Change the picture, Change the account name, Remove the password and other options to further personalise the account.

8 Click the X in the top right corner to close the window.

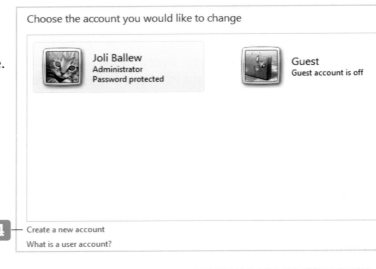

Choose the account you would like to change

Joli Ballew
Administrator
Password protected

Guest
Guest account is off

4 — Create a new account

What is a user account?

> **! ALERT:** All accounts should have a password applied to them. Refer to the next section, Require a password.

Create a password for Joli's account

Joli
Standard user

You are creating a password for Joli.

If you do this, Joli will lose all EFS-encrypted files, personal certificates and stored passwords for Web sites or network resources.

To avoid losing data in the future, ask Joli to make a password reset floppy disk.

●●●●●

●●●●●

If the password contains capital letters, they must be typed the same way every time.

How to create a strong password

Not my dog's name

The password hint will be visible to everyone who uses this computer.

What is a password hint?

[Create password] [Cancel]

? DID YOU KNOW?

Administrators can make changes to system-wide settings but Standard users cannot (without an Administrator name and password).

Require a password

All user accounts, even yours, should be password-protected. When a password is configured, you must type the password to log on to your PC or laptop. This protects the PC from unauthorised access.

1 Click Start.

2 Click Control Panel.

3 Click Add or remove user accounts.

4 Click the user account to apply a password to.

5 Click Create password.

6 Type the new password, type it again to confirm it and type a password hint.

7 Click Create password.

8 Click the X in the top right of the window to close it.

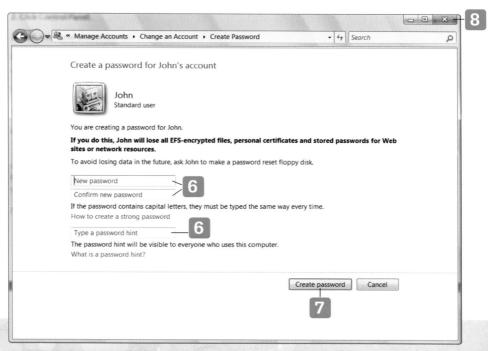

<hr/>

? DID YOU KNOW?

When you need to make a system-wide change, you have to be logged on as an administrator or type an administrator's user name and password.

! ALERT: Create a password that contains upper- and lower-case letters and a few numbers. Write the password down and keep it somewhere out of sight and safe.

Configure Windows Update

It's very important to configure Windows Update to get and install updates automatically. This is the easiest way to ensure your computer is as up to date as possible, at least as far as patching security flaws Microsoft uncovers, having access to the latest features and obtaining updates to the operating system itself. I propose you verify that the recommended settings are enabled as detailed here and occasionally check for optional updates manually.

1 Click Start.

2 Click Control Panel.

3 Click Security.

4 Click Windows Update.

5 In the left pane, click Change settings.

6 Configure the settings as shown here and click OK.

Security **3**
Check for updates
Check this computer's security status
Allow a program through Windows Firewall

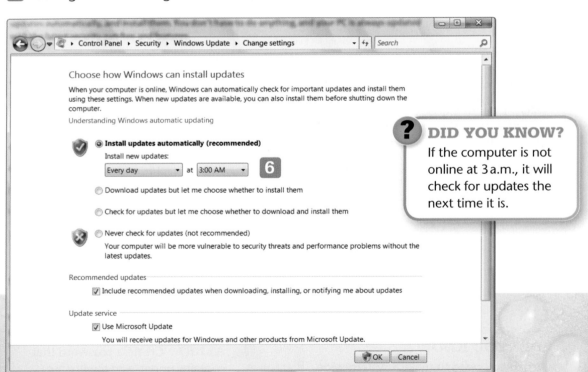

? DID YOU KNOW?
If the computer is not online at 3 a.m., it will check for updates the next time it is.

Scan for viruses with Windows Defender

You don't have to do much to Windows Defender except understand that it offers protection against Internet threats like malware. It's enabled by default and it runs in the background. However, if you ever think your computer has been attacked by an Internet threat (virus, worm, malware, etc.) you can run a manual scan here.

1 Click Start.

2 Click Control Panel.

3 Click Security.

4 Click Windows Defender.

Windows Defender
Scan for spyware and other potentially unwanted software

5 Click the arrow next to Scan (not the Scan icon).

6 Click Full Scan if you think the computer has been infected.

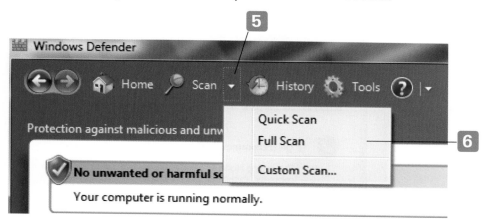

7 Click the X in the top right corner to close the Windows Defender window.

Enable the firewall

Windows Firewall is a software program that checks the data that comes in from the Internet (or a local network) and then decides whether it's good data or bad. If it deems the data harmless, it will allow it to come though the firewall; if not, it's blocked.

1 Click Start.

2 Click Control Panel.

3 Click Security.

4 Under Windows Firewall, click Turn Windows Firewall on or off.

5 Verify the firewall is on. If not, select On.

6 Click OK.

! **ALERT:** You have to have a firewall to keep hackers from getting access to your PC and to help prevent your computer from sending out malicious code if it is ever attacked by a virus or worm.

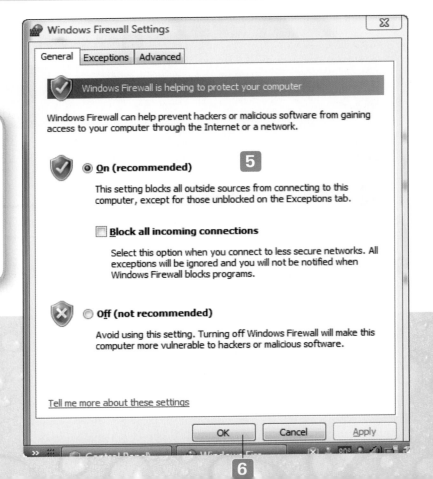

View and resolve Security Center warnings

The Security Center is a talkative application. You'll see a pop-up if your anti-virus software is out of date (or not installed), if you don't have the proper security settings configured, or if Windows Update or the Firewall is disabled. You'll also get a user account control prompt each time you want to install a program or make a system-wide change.

1 Click Start.

2 Click Control Panel.

3 Click Security.

> **ALERT:** When you see alerts like this, pay attention! You'll want to resolve them.

4 If there's anything in red or yellow, click the down arrow (if necessary) to see the problem.

5 Note the solution and perform the task.

6 Continue in this manner to resolve all Security Center-related issues.

7 Click the X in the top right corner of the Security Center window to close it.

> **? DID YOU KNOW?**
> Vista comes with malware protection but not anti-virus protection.

> **ALERT:** Install anti-virus software to protect your PC from viruses and worms.

Create a basic backup

Windows Vista comes with a backup program you can use to back up your personal data. The backup program is located in the Backup and Restore Center.

1 Click Start.

2 Click Control Panel.

3 Click Back up your computer.

4 Click Back Up Files.

5 Choose a place to save your backup. Click Next.

System and Maintenance
Get started with Windows
Back up your computer 3

HOT TIP: Since backups can be large, consider a USB drive, external hard drive or DVD. You can also choose a network location.

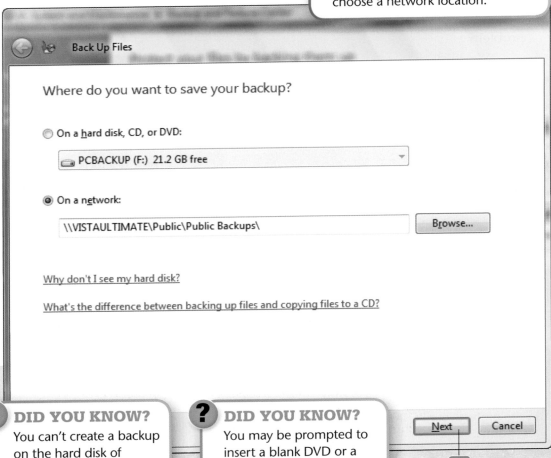

Back Up Files

Where do you want to save your backup?

○ On a hard disk, CD, or DVD:

   PCBACKUP (F:) 21.2 GB free

◉ On a network:

   \\VISTAULTIMATE\Public\Public Backups\   Browse...

Why don't I see my hard disk?

What's the difference between backing up files and copying files to a CD?

Next   Cancel

5

? DID YOU KNOW?
You can't create a backup on the hard disk of the computer you are backing up.

? DID YOU KNOW?
You may be prompted to insert a blank DVD or a USB drive depending on the choice made in step 5.

6 Select what to back up. First timers should select everything. Click Next.

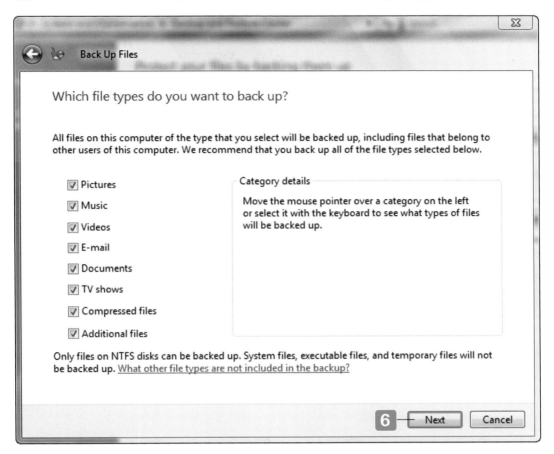

7 Choose setting for how often, what day and what time future backups should occur.

8 Click Save settings and start backup.

> ## WHAT DOES THIS MEAN?
> **Windows Update:** If enabled and configured properly, when you are online Vista will check for security updates automatically and install them. You don't have to do anything and your PC is always updated with the latest security patches and features.
> **Malware:** Stands for malicious software. Malware includes viruses, worms, spyware, etc.
> **Virus:** A self-replicating program that infects computers with intent to do harm. Viruses often come in the form of an attachment in an email.
> **Worm:** A self-replicating program that infects computers with intent to do harm. However, unlike a virus, it does not need to attach itself to a running program.

8 Install hardware

Introduction

A new PC doesn't often come with everything you need. Most of the time it does not come with a preinstalled printer or scanner, and often you buy gadgets after the fact, such as digital cameras or headphones. This hardware, as it's referred to, must be installed before it can be used. Additionally, the hardware's driver must be installed. A driver is a piece of software (or code) that allows the device to communicate with Windows Vista and vice versa. Drivers are different from software though and it's important to know the difference. In this chapter, you'll learn how to physically install printers, cameras and other hardware, and how to make them work with Windows Vista.

Install a digital camera or webcam

Most of the time, adding a camera is a simple affair. You insert the CD that came with the camera, plug in the new hardware and turn it on, and wait for Windows Vista to install your hardware. However, it's always best to have directions for performing a task, so in that vein I've included them here.

1 Read the directions that come with the camera. If there are specific instructions for installing the driver, follow them. If not, continue here.

2 Connect the camera to a wall outlet or insert fresh batteries.

3 Connect the camera to the PC using either a USB cable or a FireWire cable.

4 Insert the CD for the device, if you have it.

5 If a pop-up message appears, click the X to close the window.

6 Turn on the camera. Place it in Playback mode if that exists. Often, simply turning on the camera is enough.

7 Wait while the driver is installed.

> **ALERT:** It's usually best to connect the new camera, turn it on and let Vista install it. You need intervene only when Vista can't install the hardware on its own.

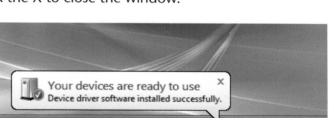

> **? DID YOU KNOW?**
> Even if you aren't installing the CD, leave the CD in the drive. If Vista wants the information on the CD, it will acquire it.

> **ALERT:** If the camera does not install properly, refer to the camera's user manual.

Install a printer

Most of the time, adding a printer is easy. You insert the CD that came with the printer, plug it in and turn it on, and wait for Windows Vista to install it. However, here are the directions for performing this task, just in case you need them.

1 Connect the printer to a wall outlet.

2 Connect the printer to the PC using either a USB cable or a parallel port cable.

3 Insert the CD for the device, if you have it.

4 If a pop-up message appears regarding the CD, click the X to close the window.

5 Turn on the device.

6 Wait while the driver is installed.

! ALERT: It's usually best to connect the new printer, turn it on and let Vista install it. You need intervene only when Vista can't install the printer on its own.

! ALERT: Always remain aware of what you're installing. Install drivers only, then install software if you find you need it.

? DID YOU KNOW?
When you install everything on the CD that comes with your printer, you're probably installing applications you'll never use and don't need.

? DID YOU KNOW?
USB is a faster connection than a parallel port, but FireWire is faster than both.

! ALERT: Read the directions that come with each new device you acquire. If there are specific instructions for installing the driver on a Vista PC, follow those directions, not the generic directions offered here.

? DID YOU KNOW?
Leave the CD in the drive. If Vista wants to access information on the CD, it will acquire it from there.

! ALERT: If the printer does not install properly, refer to the printer's user manual.

Install other hardware

For hardware other than printers or cameras, perform the same steps. Insert a driver CD if one came with the hardware, plug in the new hardware and turn it on, and wait for Windows Vista to install the required driver. If Vista can't find the driver it needs on the CD or in its own driver database on the hard drive, it will connect to the Internet and look for the driver in Microsoft's online driver database. Almost all of the time, Vista will be successful using one of these methods. For the most part, speakers, headphones, printers, scanners and digital cameras all install this way.

1 Connect the hardware to a PC and/or a wall outlet.

2 Insert the CD for the device, if you have it.

3 If a pop-up message appears regarding the CD, click the X to close the window.

4 Turn on the device.

5 Wait while the driver is installed.

ALERT: On occasion, hardware manufacturers will require you to install software first, and then plug in the device, then turn on the hardware, so read the instructions that came with your hardware to know what order to do what, just as a precaution.

ALERT: When the instruction for a hardware device tells you to install the CD before connecting the hardware, it's often just a ruse to get you to install unnecessary software, so be aware of what you're installing.

ALERT: If the hardware does not install properly, refer to the user manual.

Locate a driver

As noted, almost all of the time hardware installs automatically and with no input from you (other than plugging it in and turning it on). However, in rare cases, the hardware does not install properly or is simply not available. If this happens, you'll be informed that the hardware did not install and may not work properly. If you cannot replace the device with something Vista recognises, you'll have to locate and install the driver yourself.

1 Write down the name and model number of the device.

2 Click Start and click Internet Explorer.

3 Locate the manufacturer's website. If you find it, skip to step 5.

4 If you can't find the manufacturer's website, search for it.

5 Locate a link for Support, Support & Drivers, Customer Support or something similar. Click it.

 **DID YOU KNOW?**
If Vista can't find the drive to install the hardware, a *signed* driver may not be available.

 ALERT: When you install an unsigned driver, you take your chances. A bad driver can wreak havoc on a system, even causing it to blue-screen (or completely stop working).

HOT TIP: It's best to refrain from installing hardware that does not have a signed driver.

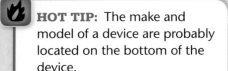 **HOT TIP:** The make and model of a device are probably located on the bottom of the device.

 HOT TIP: To find the manufacturer's website, try putting a www. before the company name and a .com after. (www.epson.com, www.hewlett-packard.com, and www.apple.com are examples).

6 Locate your device by make, model or other characteristics.

Download drivers and software

HP LaserJet 1100 Printer series

» Choose another product
» Create a personal product profile (Why register?)

By downloading, you agree to the terms and conditions of the HP Software License Agreement.

Choose your software/driver language:

English (American)

Hot topics for this product

» Learn more about Windows Vista
» HP Color LaserJet and LaserJet Printers - Drawer Statement: Microsoft Windows 98/ME Support
» Automatically check to see if your driver needs updating (MS windows only)

Select operating system

» Linux
» Microsoft MS-DOS
» Microsoft Windows 2000
» Microsoft Windows 3.0
» Microsoft Windows 3.1
» Microsoft Windows 3.11
» Microsoft Windows 95
» Microsoft Windows 98
» Microsoft Windows ME
» Microsoft Windows NT 4.0
» Microsoft Windows Server 2003
» Microsoft Windows Vista
» Microsoft Windows Vista (64-bit)
» Microsoft Windows XP
» Microsoft Windows XP 64-Bit Edition

 SEE ALSO: Open a website in Internet Explorer in Chapter 5.

 ALERT: Locating a driver is the first step. You must now download the driver, and later, install it.

Download and install a driver

If you've located the driver you need, you can now download and install it. Downloading is the process of saving the driver to your computer's hard drive. Once downloaded, you can install the driver.

1 Locate the driver as detailed in the previous section.

2 Click Download driver, Obtain software or something similar.

Driver

Description	Current version	Size (MB)	Estimated download time	Previous version	-
HP LaserJet and Color LaserJet products - products supported and drivers included in Microsoft Windows Vista	N/A 6 Dec 2006	-	-	-	» Obtain software

2

3 Click Save.

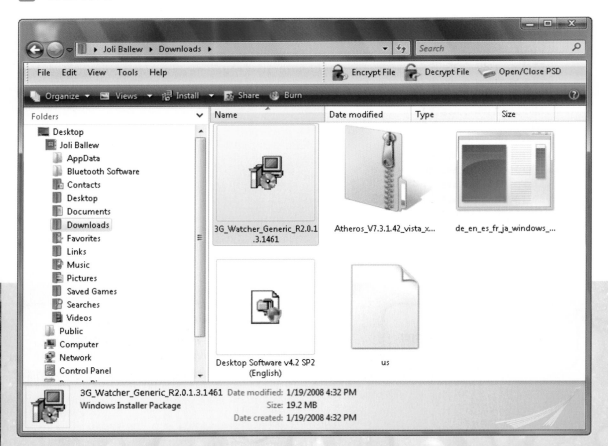

4 Click Run, Install or Open Window to begin the installation.

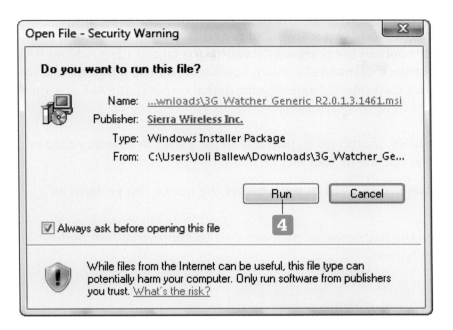

5 Follow the directions in the set-up process to complete the installation.

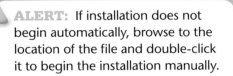 **ALERT:** If installation does not begin automatically, browse to the location of the file and double-click it to begin the installation manually.

 HOT TIP: Save the file in a location you recognise, such as Downloads.

Use ReadyBoost

ReadyBoost is a new technology that lets you add more RAM (random access memory) to a PC easily, without opening the computer tower or the laptop case. Adding RAM often improves performance dramatically. ReadyBoost lets you use a USB flash drive or a secure digital memory card (like the one in your digital camera) as RAM, if it meets certain requirements.

1 Insert a USB flash drive, thumb drive, portable music player or memory card into an available slot on the outside of your PC.

2 Wait while Windows Vista checks to see whether the device can perform as memory.

3 If prompted to use the flash drive or memory card to improve system performance, click Speed up my system.

Install software

As with installing hardware, software installation goes smoothly almost every time. Just make sure you get your software from a reliable source, such as Amazon, Microsoft's website, Apple's website or a retail store. Downloading software from the Internet is risky and you never know whether it will run properly or contain adware or spyware. It's best to simply stay away, unless the company is well known like Adobe and you're willing to burn your own software backup disks.

1 Insert the CD or DVD in the appropriate drive.

2 If prompted, choose Run.

3 If you are not prompted:

- Click Start.
- Click Computer.
- Right-click the CD or DVD drive.
- Click Install or run program.

 HOT TIP: Installing software requires you to put in the CD or DVD and follow the prompts.

 ALERT: If you aren't prompted to install the software, click Start and Computer, and manually start the installation.

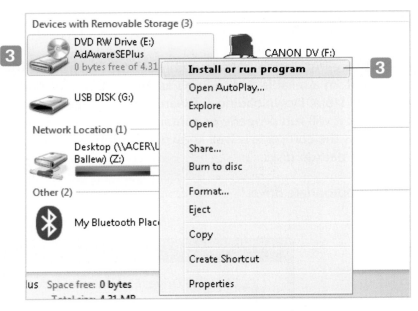

4 If prompted to cancel or allow, click Allow.

5 Work through the installation wizard.

WHAT DOES THIS MEAN?

Driver: Software that allows the PC and the new hardware to communicate with each other.

USB: A technology used to connect hardware to a PC. A USB cable is often used to connect a digital camera to a PC.

FireWire: A technology used to connect hardware to a PC. A FireWire cable is often used to connect a digital video camera to a PC.

Signed driver: A driver is signed when Microsoft has fully tested the driver for functionality.

Unsigned driver: A driver is unsigned if it has not passed Microsoft's testing process to prove it works and won't cause problems for the computer.

Search: To type a name in a website's search window in order to find something on the Internet. This term is also used to denote locating a file on a computer's hard drive.

RAM: Random access memory. RAM is where information is stored temporarily so the operating system has quick access to it. The more RAM you have, the better your PC should perform.

USB or thumb drive: Asmall device that plugs into a USB port on your PC, often for the purpose of backing up or storing files on external media.

Portable music player: Often a small USB drive. This device also has a headphone jack and controls for listening to music stored on it.

Media card: A removable card used in digital cameras to store data and transfer it to the PC.

9 Windows Media Player

Open Media Player and locate music

You open Media Player the same way you open other programs, from the Start menu. Once opened, you'll need to know where the Category button is, so you can access different kinds of media. We'll start with music.

1 Click Start.

2 Type Media Player.

3 Under Programs, click Windows Media Player to open it.

4 Click the arrow next to the Category button.

5 Click Music.

! ALERT: The first time you start Windows Media Player 11, you'll be prompted to set it up. Choose Express to accept the default settings.

? DID YOU KNOW:
By default, Music is selected.

? DID YOU KNOW:
You can select Pictures, Video or other options to access that type of media.

Listen to a song

To play any music track, simply navigate to it and double-click it. Songs are listed in the Navigation pane.

1 Open Media Player.

2 If necessary, click the Category button and choose Music.

3 Click Album. (Note you can also click Songs, Artist or any other category to locate a song.)

4 Double-click any album to play it.

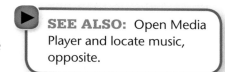

SEE ALSO: Open Media Player and locate music, opposite.

? **DID YOU KNOW?**

Media Player has Back and Forward buttons you can use to navigate Media Player.

? **DID YOU KNOW?**

The controls at the bottom of the screen from left to right are: Shuffle (to play songs in random order), Repeat, Stop, Previous, Play/Pause, Next, Mute and a volume slider.

Edit a song title and other information

Occasionally, the song title or album title won't be correct. You can edit any data related to a song or album by right-clicking it.

1 Open Media Player.

2 If necessary, click the Category button and choose Music.

3 Click Songs.

4 Right-click the song to edit.

5 Click Advanced Tag Editor.

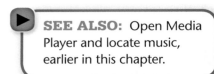

SEE ALSO: Open Media Player and locate music, earlier in this chapter.

? DID YOU KNOW?

The list that appears after right-clicking an item is called the 'shortcut menu'.

6 As desired, type a new title, select a new genre, change the album name and more.

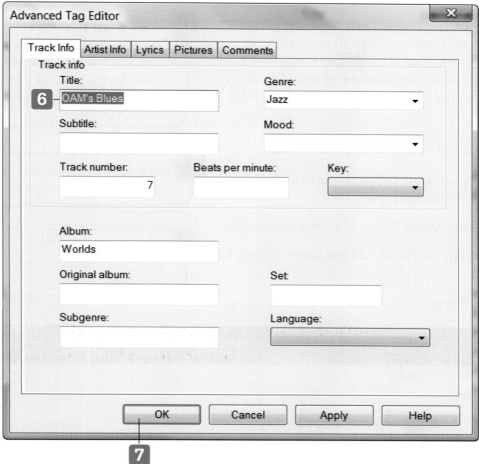

7 Click OK.

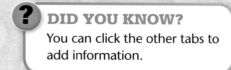

Copy a CD to your hard drive

You can copy CDs to your hard drive. This is called 'ripping'. To rip means to copy in media-speak. Once music is on your PC, you can listen to it in Media Player, burn compilations of music to other CDs and even put the music on a portable music player.

 DID YOU KNOW?
The ripped music will now appear under the Library tab under Recently Added, as well as in Artist, Album, Songs, Genre and Year.

1 Insert the CD to copy into the CD drive.

2 If any pop-up boxes appear, click the X to close out of them.

 HOT TIP: You can watch the rip progress in the List pane.

3 In Windows Media Player, click the Rip button.

4 Deselect any songs you do not want to copy to your PC.

 DID YOU KNOW?
By default, music is saved in your Music folder.

5 Click Start Rip.

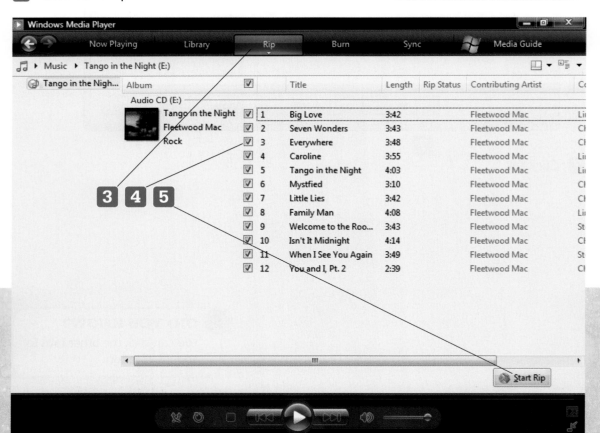

Create a playlist

Playlists allow you to organise songs the way you like to listen to them. You might consider creating playlists that contain songs specific to an occasion, such as a dinner party, after-pub party, engagement party, or similar event. Then, when the event happens, you can simply put on the playlist and let the music take care of itself.

1. Open Windows Media Player.

2. Click Create Playlist.

3. When you click Create Playlist, the type will turn blue. Type the name of the playlist here.

4. The new playlist name will appear under Playlists. Click it. Note: When you click the new playlist, it will appear in the List pane.

5. Click Recently Added, Artist, Album, Songs, Genre and Year as needed to locate the songs to add to the playlist.

6. Drag those songs to the Playlists Pane.

7. Continue to drag and drop songs.

8. When finished, click Save Playlist.

ALERT: Lost? Click the Library tab.

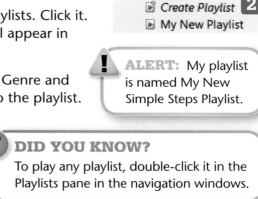

ALERT: My playlist is named My New Simple Steps Playlist.

? DID YOU KNOW?
To play any playlist, double-click it in the Playlists pane in the navigation windows.

Copy music files to a CD

There are two ways to take music with you when you are on the road or on the go. You can copy the music to a portable device like a music player, or you can create your own CDs, choosing the songs to copy and placing them on the CD in the desired order.

? DID YOU KNOW?
CDs you create in Media Player can be played in car stereos and portable CD players, as well as on lots of other CD devices.

1 Open Media Player.

2 Click the arrow under the Burn tab.

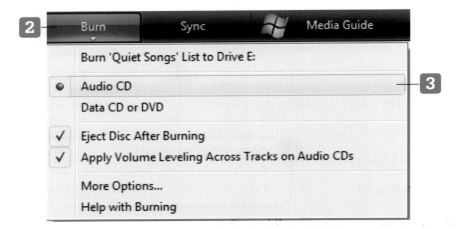

3 Verify Audio CD has a dot by it. If it does not, click it once.

4 Verify that Apply Volume Leveling Across Tracks on Audio CDs has a tick by it.

5 Click outside the drop-down list to close it.

6 Insert a blank CD in the CD drive. (Close out of any pop-up dialogue boxes.)

7 Under Library, click Songs or Album.

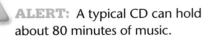

! ALERT: A typical CD can hold about 80 minutes of music.

? DID YOU KNOW?
Media Player will keep track of the songs you select and will let you know when you're running out of space on the CD you are creating.

8 Click any song title or album to add, and drag it to the List pane.

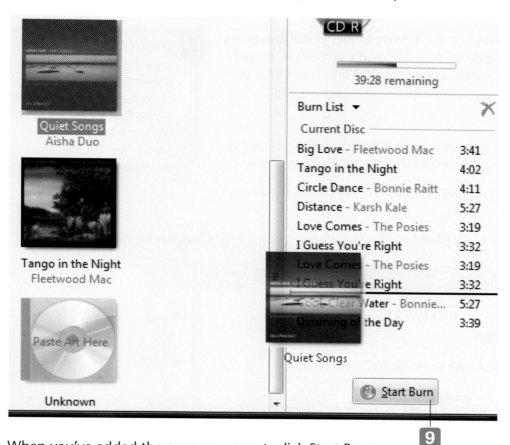

9 When you've added the songs you want, click Start Burn.

? DID YOU KNOW?
Look at the slider in the List pane to see how much room is left on the CD.

? DID YOU KNOW?
You can right-click any entry to access additional options including Remove from List, Move Up, Move Down.

 HOT TIP: You can drag and drop playlists too. There will be more information on playlists later in this chapter.

Watch a DVD

You can watch a DVD on your computer just as you would on any DVD player. Vista offers two choices for doing so, Windows Media Center and Windows Media Player. We'll talk about Windows Media Player here.

 DID YOU KNOW?
If you have Windows Vista Home Premium or Vista Ultimate, you have Windows Media *Center*. It's best to watch DVDs in Media Center, not Media Player, if you have it.

1 Find the button on the PC's tower, keyboard or laptop that opens the DVD drive door. Press it.

2 Place the DVD in the door and press the button again to close it.

3 When prompted, choose Play DVD movie using Windows Media Player.

 SEE ALSO: If the DVD plays automatically and no choice is offered, refer to Change AutoPlay settings in Chapter 12.

HOT TIP: The controls you'll see and use in Media Player are very similar to (and perhaps exactly like) the controls you see on your own DVD player.

WHAT DOES THIS MEAN?

Windows Media Player: An application included with every Windows Vista edition. You will watch DVDs and videos here if you have Windows Vista Basic or Vista Business. If you have Home Premium or Ultimate, you'll probably opt to watch DVDs in Media Center, because it's a more comprehensive media application.

Advanced Tag Editor: A dialogue box where you can edit the information about a song or album (or other data).

Visualizations: These are graphical representations of the music you play. You can turn them off or on, and there are several to choose from. These Visualizations move with the music and are computer generated.

Enhancements: These are features included in Media Player 11 which let you change the song's speed, apply equalisation, apply auto volume levelling and more.

Graphic Equallizer: An enhancement that lets you select optimal settings for the type of music you listen to or create your own equalisation settings.

Burn: A term used to describe the process of copying music from a computer to a CD.

Volume Levelling: Makes all songs on the CD record at the same volume so that some tracks are not louder (or softer) than others.

Display media information from the Internet: Leave this option selected if you want Media Player to access the Internet to display information about the media you are watching or listening to. I see no reason to deselect this unless you have an extremely slow Internet connection or pay by how much bandwidth you use.

Update music files by retrieving media information from the Internet: Deselect this option if you have an existing media library that you've added your own data to, such as album art, artist names and other data. If this is the first time you've used Media Player, leave this option selected. You media will be updated automatically.

Download usage rights automatically when I play a file: Leave this option selected; you don't want to worry about usage rights when Media Player can manage it for you.

Send unique Player ID to content providers: Leave this unticked. If you tick it, media providers can uniquely identify your computer when you use their media servers. Although this can improve performance, in my opinion it's an invasion of privacy.

I want to help make Microsoft software and services even better by sending Player usage data to Microsoft: Select this option to help Microsoft improve later editions of Media Player, otherwise don't select it. No personally identifiable information will be sent to Microsoft either way.

Save file and URL history in the Player: Leave this ticked if you want to save your history in the Player. This allows the Player to display recently played files on the File menu and in the Open and Open URL dialogue boxes. It's simply a convenience. Deselect this if others have access to your account and you do not want them to see what you've been listening to or watching.

10 Windows Photo Gallery

View pictures

You can use various applications to view pictures with Vista, but Windows Photo Gallery is the best. With it, you have easy access to slide shows, editing tools and picture groupings. You can sort and filter and organise as desired.

1 Click Start.

2 Type Photo Gallery in the Start Search window.

3 From the Start results, under Programs, click Windows Photo Gallery.

4 In the View pane, expand the Folders tree and then the Pictures tree.

5 Select any folder name.

6 Hover the mouse over any picture to see a larger thumbnail of it.

7 Click Pictures at the top of the View window.

8 Click the X to close Windows Photo Gallery.

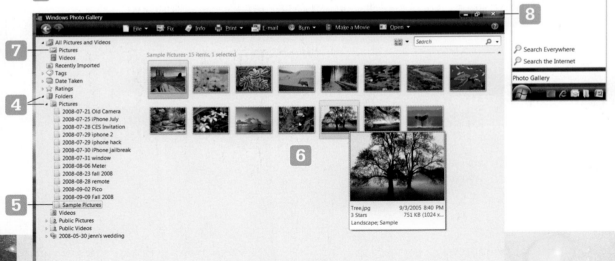

Import pictures from a digital camera

After you've taken pictures with your digital camera, you'll want to move or copy those pictures to the PC. Once stored on the PC's hard drive, you can view, edit, email or print the pictures (among other things).

1 Connect the device. If applicable, turn it on.

2 When prompted, choose Import Pictures using Windows.

3 Type a descriptive name for the group of pictures you're importing.

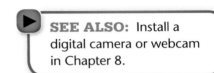

SEE ALSO: Install a digital camera or webcam in Chapter 8.

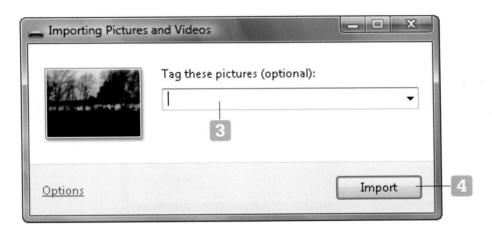

4 Click Import.

? **DID YOU KNOW?**
These steps work for importing pictures from a mobile phone too.

HOT TIP: If desired, tick Erase after importing. This will cause Vista to erase the images from the device after the import is complete.

! **ALERT:** If your device isn't recognised when you plug it in and turn it on, in Windows Photo Gallery click File, then click Import from Camera or Scanner.

Import pictures from a media card

If your digital camera has a media card and your PC has a built-in media card reader, you can insert the card into the reader and import pictures. You do not have to connect the camera or turn it on.

1 Remove the media card from the camera and insert it into the media card reader.

2 When prompted, choose Import Pictures using Windows.

3 Type a descriptive name for the group of pictures you're importing.

4 Click Import. You can see progress as below.

Play a slideshow of pictures

1. Open Windows Photo Gallery.

2. Expand any folder that contains pictures.

3. Click the Play Slide Show button. Wait at least three seconds.

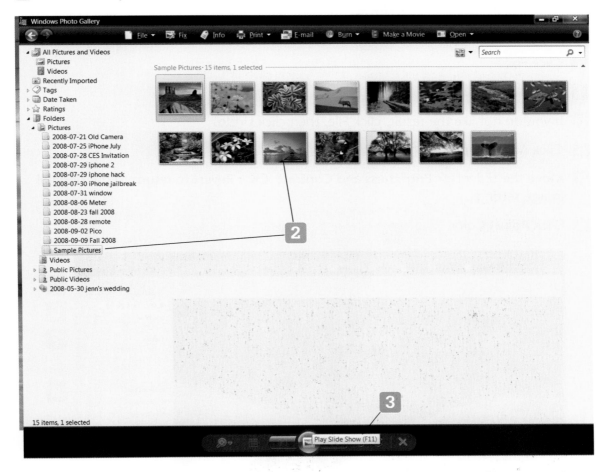

4. To end the show, press the Esc key on the keyboard.

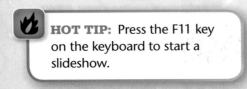

HOT TIP: Press the F11 key on the keyboard to start a slideshow.

Auto adjust picture quality

With pictures on your PC and available in Windows Photo Gallery, you can now perform some editing. Photo Gallery offers the ability to correct brightness and contrast, colour temperature, tint and saturation, among other things.

1 Open Photo Gallery.

2 Double-click a picture to edit.

3 Click Fix.

4 Click Auto Adjust.

5 If you do not like the result, click File, then click Undo.

6 Click Adjust Exposure.

7 Move the sliders for Brightness and Contrast. Click Revert to return to the original image settings.

8 Click Adjust Color.

9 Move the sliders for Color Temperature, Tint and Saturation. Click Revert to Original to return to the original image settings.

10 To save changes and work on another picture, click Back to Gallery.

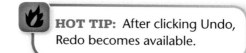
HOT TIP: After clicking Undo, Redo becomes available.

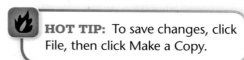
HOT TIP: At any time during the editing process you can revert to the original picture. Click File, and click Revert to Original.

HOT TIP: To save changes, click File, then click Make a Copy.

ALERT: Click Back To Gallery to return to the picture gallery (the previous screen).

Fix red eye

The Fix Red Eye tool lets you draw a rectangle around any eye that has a red dot in it and the red dot is automatically removed.

1 Open Photo Gallery.

2 Double-click a picture to edit.

3 Click Fix.

4 Click Fix Red Eye.

5 Drag the mouse over the red part of the eye. When you let go, the red eye in the picture will be removed.

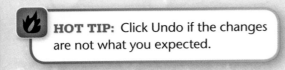

HOT TIP: Click Undo if the changes are not what you expected.

Crop a picture

To crop means to remove parts of a picture you don't want by allowing you to reposition the picture and remove extraneous parts. You can also rotate the frame.

1 Open Photo Gallery.

2 Select a picture to crop.

3 Click Fix.

4 Click Crop Picture.

5 Drag the corners of the box to resize it and drag the entire box to move it around in the picture.

6 Click Apply.

HOT TIP: Click the arrow next to Custom to apply a preconfigured size.

HOT TIP: Click Rotate Frame to change the position of the crop box.

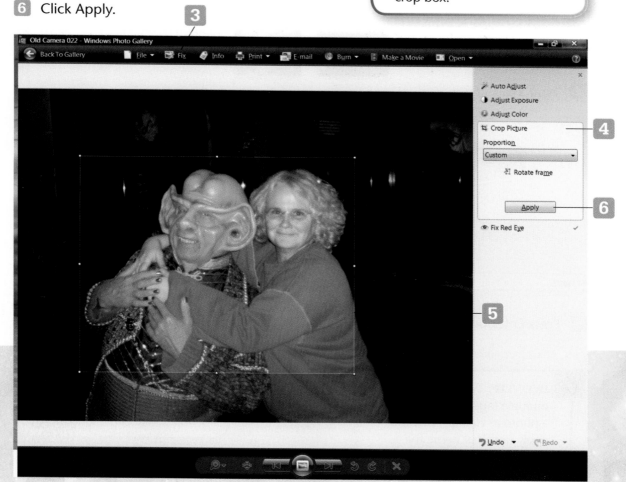

Add information to a picture

You can add information about a picture by adding 'tags'. Tags you create are words that describe the picture. Once tags are added, you can filter, sort and organise your pictures using these tags.

1 Open Windows Photo Gallery.

2 Right-click any picture.

3 Click Add Tags.

Preview Picture
Open With ▶
Set as Desktop Background
Open File Location
Add Tags...
Clear Rating
Rotate Clockwise
Rotate Counterclockwise
Change Time Taken...
Copy
Delete
Rename...
Properties

4 Type a tag name.

Picture 063.JPG
7/24/2005 3:30 PM
265 KB (1280 x 960)
☆☆☆☆☆

4 — Chairs

5 Press Enter on the keyboard.

HOT TIP: Pictures can have multiple tags. You might tag a photo as Holiday, but also apply tags that name the people in the picture, the city or the country.

HOT TIP: To remove the tag (or any other tag), click Remove tag.

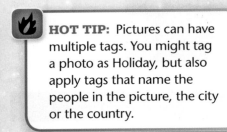

Email a picture

You can email photos you want to share from inside Photo Gallery. You can also choose the size to email them – I suggest either Small or Medium (for best results).

1 Open Windows Photo Gallery.

2 Select pictures to email.

3 Click E-mail.

4 Select a picture size.

5 Click Attach.

6 Compose the email and send it.

? DID YOU KNOW?
The larger the image, the longer it will take to send and receive.

▶ SEE ALSO: Compose and send a new email in Chapter 6.

🔥 HOT TIP: For email, generally 800 × 600 is best. It's small enough to be sent and received quickly, even on dial-up, and it fits nicely in the recipient's Inbox.

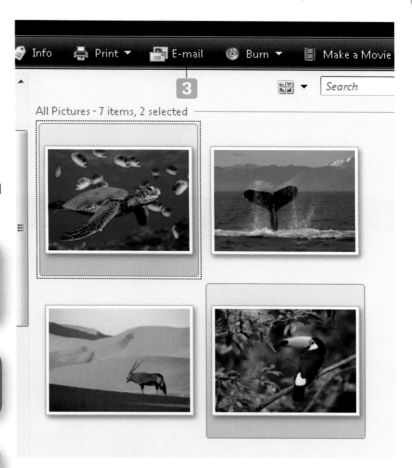

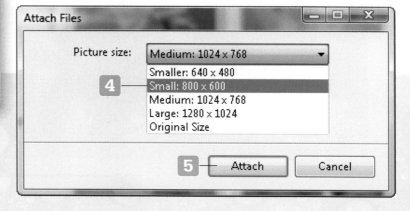

Print a picture

You can share a picture by printing it. Again, you can print from inside Photo Gallery.

1 Open Photo Gallery.

2 Select a picture to print. (You can also double-click the image as I've done here.)

3 Click Print.

4 Click Print again.

5 Using the Print Pictures wizard, select the type and number of prints to create.

6 Click Print.

? **DID YOU KNOW?**
You can click Order prints online to get prints delivered to you using an online printing company.

 HOT TIP: Edit the picture first for best results.

WHAT DOES THIS MEAN?

View pane: The pane to the left is the View pane, where you'll select the folder or subfolder that contains the pictures you want to view, manage, edit or share.

Expand a tree: Click the right-facing arrow to show the contents of a folder.

Thumbnail pane: The pane on the right, where you preview the pictures in the folder selected in the View pane.

Media card: A small card that holds data in digital devices such as cameras.

Media card reader: A slot usually in the side of a laptop or the front of a PC or printer that allows you to insert a media card and retrieve the information on it.

Auto Adjust: This tool automatically assesses the image and alters it, which, most of the time results in a better image. However, there's always the Undo button and you'll probably use it on occasion.

Adjust Exposure: This tool offers slider controls for Brightness and Contrast. You move these sliders to the left and right to adjust as desired.

Adjust Color: This tool offers slider controls to adjust the temperature, tint and saturation of the photo. Temperature runs from blue to yellow, allowing you to change the 'atmosphere' of the image. Tint runs from green to red and saturation moves from black and white to colour.

Red eye: The result of a flash reflecting in the eyes of the subject.

11 Windows Media Center

Introduction

Windows Media Center is included with both Windows Vista Home Premium and Windows Vista Ultimate editions. Media Center is a one-stop media application that lets you access and manage pictures, videos, movies, music, online media, television, DVDs and CDs, and radio.

Media Center really stands out for watching cable and Internet TV and online media, and watching DVDs you own or rent. It's a 'media centre' if you will, a place to enjoy the media you already have access to and have already 'managed' in other applications (such as Photo Gallery or Media Player). Media Center has an online TV guide to help you find out what's available to watch and when, and you can record television programmes, pause live TV, and then fast-forward or rewind through what you've paused and recorded.

You should start with Media Center by watching and recording TV, then move on to watching DVDs and viewing online media. As time passes and you become more comfortable with Media Center, you may find you prefer it over Media Player and Photo Gallery for managing other media too.

Open Media Center

1 Click Start.

2 Click All Programs.

3 Click Media Center.

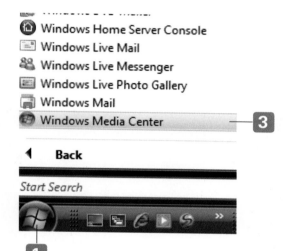

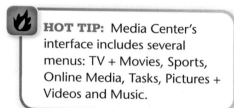

HOT TIP: Media Center's interface includes several menus: TV + Movies, Sports, Online Media, Tasks, Pictures + Videos and Music.

Set up Media Center

The first time you open Media Center, you'll be prompted to set it up. You'll need to configure several things: Internet connection, TV signal, speakers and your TV or monitor. You may also see the option to join a wireless network.

! ALERT: As it's nearly impossible to detail here how to set up Media Center because of the sheer number of options, a generic introduction is offered.

1 Open Media Center.

2 When you see the set-up screen shown here, start at the top and work your way down.

? DID YOU KNOW?
Setup walks you through each process, giving you options, pictures and diagrams to help you make the correct choices.

! ALERT: Although some set-up options are not required, it's best to work through all of them.

▶ SEE ALSO: If you stop Setup before you complete each item, refer to the following section, Restart Setup.

Restart Setup

If you did not complete the Media Center set-up tasks or if you'd like to make changes to the current configuration, you can restart Setup.

1 Start Media Center.

2 Position the mouse below the menu options and click to scroll. Stop at Tasks.

3 Once at Tasks, click Settings.

4 In the Settings options, click General.

5 From the General options, click Windows Media Center Setup.

? DID YOU KNOW?

There are several ways to open Media Center. Just look for the Media Center icon on a remote control or keyboard, or locate it on the Start Menu, in a shortcut, or even in the Quick Launch area of the toolbar (you can drag it there from the Start menu).

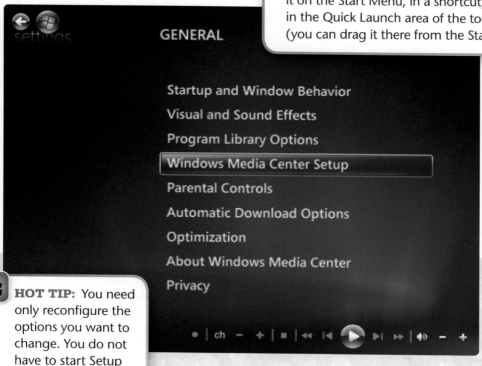

HOT TIP: You need only reconfigure the options you want to change. You do not have to start Setup over again.

Watch, pause and rewind live TV

When you open Media Center, TV + Movies is the default option and Recorded TV is selected. To watch live television, you'll need to use the mouse or remote control to move to the right of recorded TV to live TV. While watching live TV, you can watch, pause and rewind the show you're watching (and fast-forward through previously paused programming).

1 Open Media Center.

2 Move to the right of recorded TV once and click live tv.

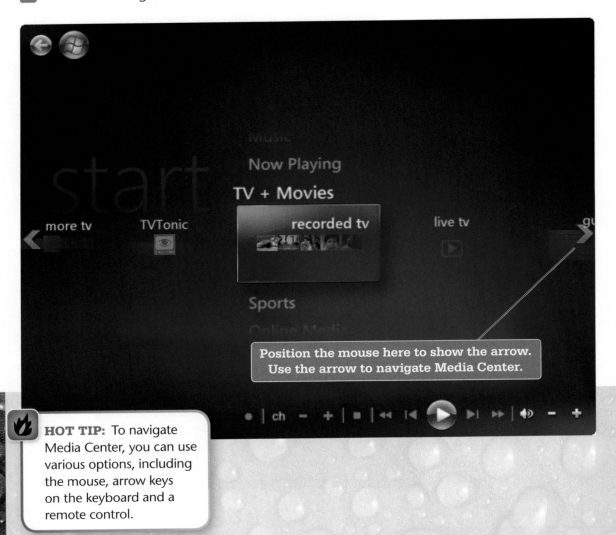

Position the mouse here to show the arrow.
Use the arrow to navigate Media Center.

HOT TIP: To navigate Media Center, you can use various options, including the mouse, arrow keys on the keyboard and a remote control.

3 Position the mouse at the bottom of the live TV screen to show the controls.

4 Use the controls to manage live TV.

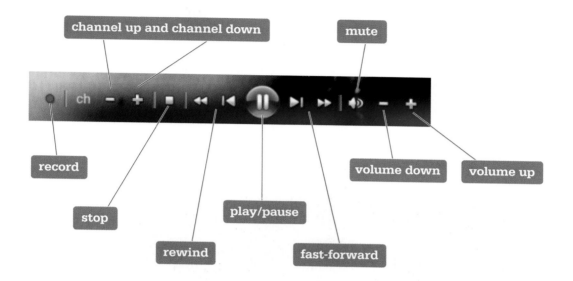

channel up and channel down

mute

record

volume down

volume up

stop

play/pause

rewind

fast-forward

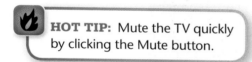 **HOT TIP:** Mute the TV quickly by clicking the Mute button.

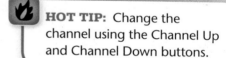 **HOT TIP:** Change the channel using the Channel Up and Channel Down buttons.

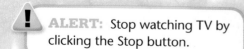 **ALERT:** Stop watching TV by clicking the Stop button.

 HOT TIP: Press pause at the beginning of a 30-minute show for 10 minutes and you can fast-forward through the commercials. (For a 60-minute show, pause for 20 minutes.)

Record a future TV show

There are a lot of ways to access the commands to Record and Record Series, including right-clicking while watching a live TV show. You won't always want to record what you're watching though; it is more likely that you will want to record something that is coming on later in the week. That's what the guide is for.

1 Open Media Center.

2 Under TV + Movies, move right and click guide.

3 Locate a show to record.

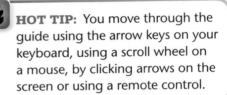

HOT TIP: You move through the guide using the arrow keys on your keyboard, using a scroll wheel on a mouse, by clicking arrows on the screen or using a remote control.

4 Click the programme.

5 Select Record.

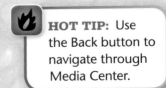

HOT TIP: Use the Back button to navigate through Media Center.

Watch a recorded TV show

To watch a television show you've recorded, simply browse to TV + Movies, Recorded TV and click the recorded show you want to watch!

1. Open Media Center and under TV + Movies, click recorded TV.

2. Locate the programme to watch.

3. Click Play.

 HOT TIP: While accessing recorded TV, you can also add a recording, view scheduled recordings and browse by title or date.

3

2

program info

Play

Delete

Keep Until

Record Series

Other Showings

Burn CD/DVD

Stargate SG-1
65 SCIFI-Sci-Fi Channel
Recorded 9/26, 10:00 AM - 11:00 AM

"Bad Guys" - SG-1 team members must play the part of hostage-takers when inhabitants of an alien planet mistake them for rebels.

Beau Bridges, Michael Shanks, Amanda Tapping, Christopher Judge, Ben Browder

Original air date: 5/18/2007, Series/Other, TV-PG, CC, 60 minutes, English, TV-PG L

Keep until I watch

? **DID YOU KNOW?**
When you record a series, a folder will be created for it that will hold the related shows.

 HOT TIP: You can pause, rewind and fast-forward a recorded TV show in the same manner as watching live TV.

View your pictures

Although you can use Windows Photo Gallery to view your pictures, you may find you like Media Center better.

1 Open Media Center.

2 Scroll to Pictures + Videos and click picture library.

3 Browse through the available pictures and picture folders.

4 Click play slide show to play a slideshow of the pictures in that folder.

 HOT TIP: Position the mouse at the bottom of the screen to show the controls.

Watch a DVD

You know you can watch a DVD in Media Player, and you can also watch a DVD in Media Center.

1 Put a DVD in the DVD drive.

2 If prompted, choose Play DVD movie using Windows Media Center.

3 Use the mouse, remote control or arrow on the keyboard to play the movie, view special features or select other options.

4 Use the controls introduced earlier to pause, stop, rewind and fast-forward through the movie.

? DID YOU KNOW?

You can also browse to TV + Movies in Media Center and from the submenus choose play dvd.

Listen to music

You know you can listen to music in Media Player, and you can also listen to music in Media Center.

1 Open Media Center.

2 Scroll to Music and click music library.

3 Locate the album to play.

4 Click Play Album or select any other option.

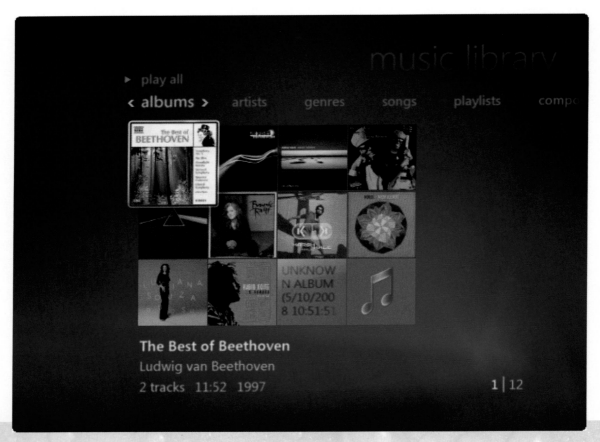

? DID YOU KNOW?
You can click artists, genres, songs, playlists and more to refine the list.

WHAT DOES THIS MEAN?

Settings: Access to change Media Center-wide settings for TV, Pictures, Music & DVDs.

Shutdown: Choose from Close (to close Media Center), Log off (to log off the computer), Shut Down, Restart and Sleep.

Burn CD/DVD: Access options to burn various types of audio and data CDs and DVDs.

Sync: Click to sync a portable device such as a Zune (a Zune is a portable music player, similar to the iPod and competing portable devices).

Add Extender: Access the Media Center Extender Setup wizard to connect an extender to the computer and configure options. Extenders let you share media throughout your home.

Media Only: Anything you watch will appear in full-screen mode.

Recorded TV: Click to access TV shows you've recorded.

Live TV and/or Internet TV: View Live or Internet TV.

Movies Guide: View movies.

Play DVD: Watch a DVD you have.

Search: Search for media by title, keyword, category, actor or director.

Program Info: Displays the Program Info screen where you can record the programme, the series and acquire information about the show.

Record: Immediately starts recording the current television show.

Record Series: Immediately starts recording the current television show and schedules the television series to be recorded.

Zoom: Changes how the picture is displayed.

Mini Guide: Shows information about the show on the screen in a minimised format (at least compared with Program Info).

Settings: Opens Media Center Settings.

Record: Schedule a television show to record the next time it airs. Once scheduled to record, a red dot will appear in the guide for that programme.

Record Series: Schedule an entire series to record. As with Record, a red dot will appear in the guide for that programme.

More Pictures: Access pictures from the Internet.

Picture Library: View the images on your computer, including those on a CD or DVD, and shared pictures on the network.

Play All: View a slide show of the pictures on your PC.

Video Library: Access videos stored on the PC or network drives.

More Music: Access music on the Internet.

Music Library: Access your music and playlists created in Media Player 11, or search for music by various criteria.

Play All: Play the music in your music library and change the order songs are played, Visualizations, shuffle music, repeat songs and buy music.

Radio: Access local radio stations and configure presets.

Search: Search for the music you want.

12 Change system defaults

Change AutoPlay settings

Vista doesn't know what you want it to do when you insert a blank CD, a DVD movie or even a music CD, so most of the time it asks you by offering up a dialogue box. You can tell Vista what you want it to do when you insert or access media though, thus bypassing the prompt and getting right to the music, picture or DVD you want to view.

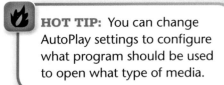 **HOT TIP:** You can change AutoPlay settings to configure what program should be used to open what type of media.

1 Click Start.

2 Click Default Programs on the Start menu.

3 Click Change AutoPlay settings.

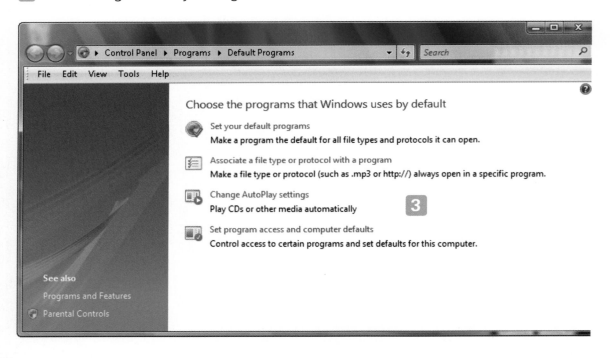

4 Use the drop-down lists to select the program to use for the media you want to play.

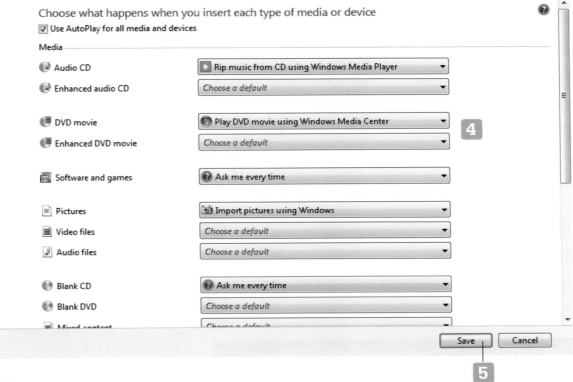

5 Click Save.

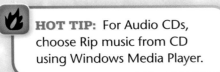

HOT TIP: For Audio CDs, choose Rip music from CD using Windows Media Player.

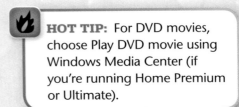

HOT TIP: For DVD movies, choose Play DVD movie using Windows Media Center (if you're running Home Premium or Ultimate).

Change the date and time

If there is ever a need to change the date and time (or the time zone), you can do so from the Date and Time dialogue box.

1 Click Start.

2 Click Control Panel.

3 Click Clock, Language, and Region.

4 Click Set the time and date.

Date and Time **4**
Set the time and date | Change the time zone | Add clocks for different time zones
Add the Clock gadget to Windows Sidebar

5 Click Change date and time.

6 Use the arrows or type in a new time.

7 Select a new date.

8 Click OK.

9 Click OK.

HOT TIP: Click the Additional Clocks tab to add a second clock in a different time zone.

HOT TIP: Choose Change time zone to change the time zone instead of the time.

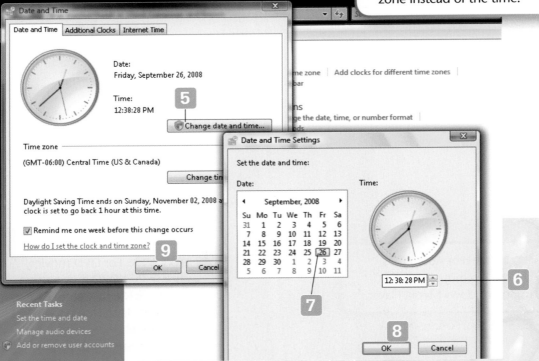

Change language settings

When you travel with a laptop, you may need to change the country or region, the date, time and number format. If you speak and work in multiple languages, you may also need to change keyboards or other input methods. You can do this from the Control Panel.

1 Click Start.

2 Click Control Panel.

3 Click Clock, Language, and Region.

4 Click Regional and Language Options.

5 Make changes as desired from the available drop-down lists.

6 Click OK.

 DID YOU KNOW?
You can customise any format by clicking the Customize this format button.

HOT TIP: To set your current location, click the Current Location tab and select the desired country from the drop-down list.

Change folder options

You can change how folders react using Folder Options. You can use a single-click (instead of a double-click) to open a folder, choose to open each folder in its own window, view hidden files and folders and more.

1 Click Start.

2 In the Start Search window, type Folder Options.

3 Under Programs in the results list, click Folder Options.

4 From the General tab, read the options and make changes as desired.

5 From the View tab, read the options and make changes as desired.

6 From the Search tab, read the options and make changes as desired.

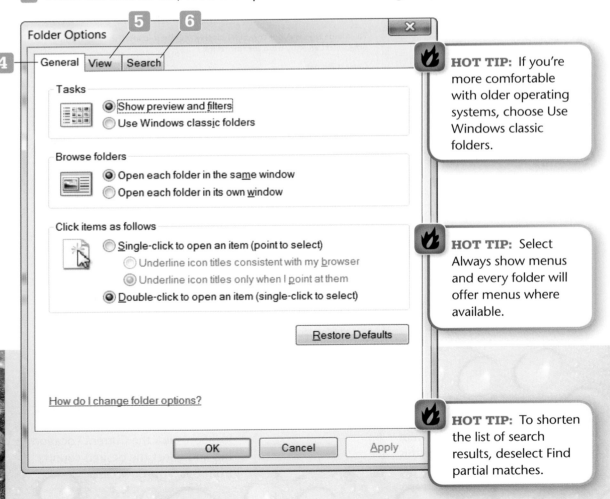

HOT TIP: If you're more comfortable with older operating systems, choose Use Windows classic folders.

HOT TIP: Select Always show menus and every folder will offer menus where available.

HOT TIP: To shorten the list of search results, deselect Find partial matches.

Change mouse settings

The speed the mouse moves, the pointer shape, vertical scrolling and other mouse options are all configured with default settings. You can change the settings, perhaps turning a right-handed mouse into a left-handed mouse using Mouse settings.

1. Click Start and in the Start Search window, type mouse.

2. In the results, under Programs, click Mouse.

3. From the Buttons tab, read the options and make changes as desired.

4. From the Pointers tab, select a theme as desired.

5. From the Pointer Options tab, read the options and make changes as desired.

6. From the Wheel tab, read the options and make changes as desired.

7. Click OK.

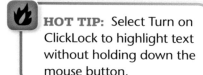

HOT TIP: Select Turn on ClickLock to highlight text without holding down the mouse button.

HOT TIP: Just for fun, try the Dinosaur theme. When the computer is busy, the mouse pointer will look like a dinosaur instead of the default moving, blue circle.

HOT TIP: If you're not happy with how fast the pointer moves when you move your mouse, you can change that speed here.

HOT TIP: Enable Snap To and the mouse will move to the default option in dialogue boxes.

HOT TIP: To scroll an entire screen at a time instead of three lines at a time, select One screen at a time.

Change when the computer sleeps

You computer is configured to go to sleep after a specific period of idle time. If you do not want your computer to go to sleep, for instance if Media Center is supposed to record something in the middle of the night, you can change this behaviour.

1 Click Start and in the Start Search window type Power.

2 In the results, under Programs, click Power Options.

3 Click Change when the computer sleeps.

4 Use the drop-down lists to make changes as desired.

5 Click Save changes.

? DID YOU KNOW?
You can restore the sleep defaults by clicking Restore default settings for this plan.

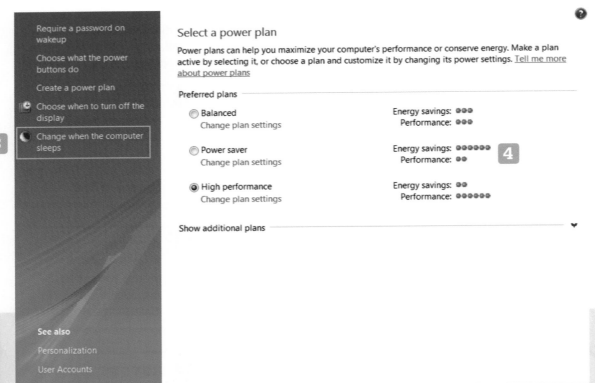

Require a password on wakeup

Choose what the power buttons do

Create a power plan

Choose when to turn off the display

3 Change when the computer sleeps

Select a power plan

Power plans can help you maximize your computer's performance or conserve energy. Make a plan active by selecting it, or choose a plan and customize it by changing its power settings. Tell me more about power plans

Preferred plans

○ Balanced
  Change plan settings

Energy savings: ●●●
Performance: ●●●

○ Power saver
  Change plan settings

Energy savings: ●●●●●●
Performance: ●●

4

◉ High performance
  Change plan settings

Energy savings: ●●
Performance: ●●●●●●

Show additional plans

See also

Personalization

User Accounts

Change what happens when you press the Power button

Your computer is configured to do something specific when you press the Power button. By default, this is to shut down the computer, but you can change this behaviour.

1 Click Start and in the Start Search window type Power.

2 In the results, under Programs, click Power Options.

3 Click Choose what the power buttons do.

4 Use the drop-down lists to make changes as desired.

5 Click Save changes.

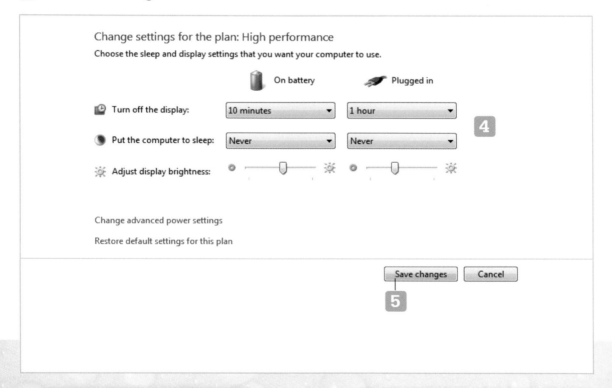

Change settings for the plan: High performance
Choose the sleep and display settings that you want your computer to use.

	On battery	Plugged in
Turn off the display:	10 minutes	1 hour
Put the computer to sleep:	Never	Never
Adjust display brightness:		

4

Change advanced power settings
Restore default settings for this plan

Save changes   Cancel

5

HOT TIP: You can change the settings so that pressing the Power button causes the computer to go to sleep.

ALERT: You can also require a password when the computer resumes from sleep to protect your PC from unauthorised access.

13 Share data and printers

Open the Network and Sharing Center

The Network and Sharing Center is where you tell Vista what you want to share with others on your network.

1 Click Start.

2 In the Start Search window, type Network and Sharing.

3 Under Programs, click Network and Sharing Center.

4 The Network and Sharing Center opens.

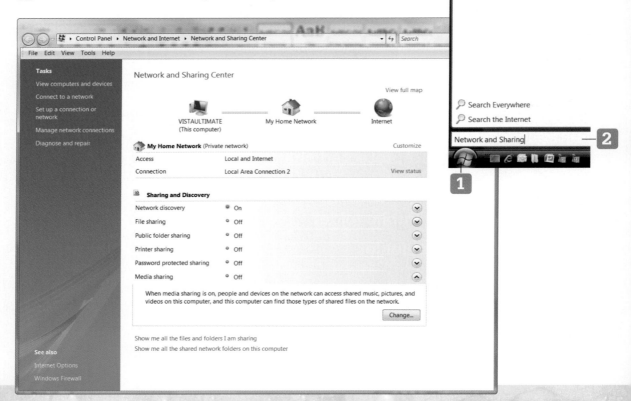

? **DID YOU KNOW?**
You can also simply type Network in the Start Search window.

? **DID YOU KNOW?**
Network Discovery must be turned on in order for your PC to find other PCs and to share data.

! **ALERT:** Notice the down arrows in the list. Clicking them offers more information about each section.

Turn on file sharing

When you turn on file sharing, files and folders on your PC that you have shared are accessible by others on your local network.

1 Open the Network and Sharing Center.

2 Click the down arrow by File sharing.

3 Click Turn on file sharing.

4 Click Apply.

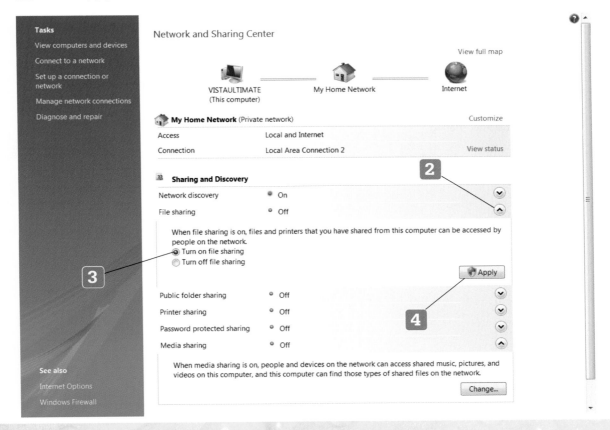

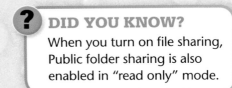

? DID YOU KNOW?

When you turn on file sharing, Public folder sharing is also enabled in "read only" mode.

Turn on printer sharing

When you turn on printer sharing, printers you have shared are accessible by others on your local network. You must turn on printer sharing for other PCs to obtain access to your shared printers.

1 Open the Network and Sharing Center.

2 Click the down arrow by Printer sharing.

3 Click Turn on printer sharing.

4 Click Apply.

HOT TIP: Click Start and in the Start Search window, type Printers. You can then open the Printers folder to manage shared printers.

SEE ALSO: Share a printer (next).

Share a printer

After turning on printer sharing, you'll need to manually share the printer(s) you want others to have access to.

1 Click Start, and in the Start Search window, type Printers.

2 Under Programs, click Printers.

3 Locate the printer to share.

4 Right-click the printer, click Sharing.

5 Click Share this printer.

6 Click OK.

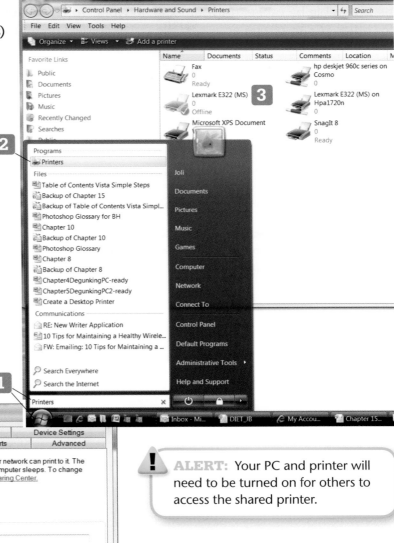

ALERT: Your PC and printer will need to be turned on for others to access the shared printer.

ALERT: When others on your network access the printer for the first time, they may be prompted to install a driver for it. This is OK and will be managed by the PC.

Turn on Public folder sharing

When you turn on public folder sharing, data you have saved in the Public folders will be accessible by others on your local network. You must turn on public folder sharing for other PCs to obtain access to the Public folders on your PC.

1 Open the Network and Sharing Center.

2 Click the down arrow by Public folder sharing.

3 Make a sharing selection.

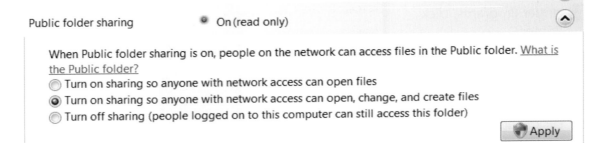

4 Click Apply.

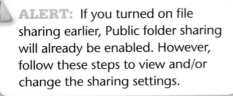

ALERT: If you turned on file sharing earlier, Public folder sharing will already be enabled. However, follow these steps to view and/or change the sharing settings.

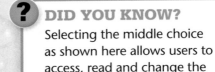

DID YOU KNOW?
Selecting the middle choice as shown here allows users to access, read and change the data inside the Public folders.

Turn on password-protected sharing

When password-protected sharing is on, only people who have a user account and a password on the computer can access shared files and printers. If you want all users to input a user name and password, enable this feature.

1 Open the Network and Sharing Center.

2 Click the down arrow by Password-protected sharing.

3 Click Turn on password protected sharing and click Apply.

Password protected sharing On

> When password protection is on, only people who have a user account and password on this computer can access shared files, printers attached to this computer, and the Public folder. To give other people access, you must turn off password protection.
> ● Turn on password protected sharing
> ○ Turn off password protected sharing

! ALERT: Users who have a user name but not a password will not be able to access files until they apply a password to their account.

! ALERT: This feature does not have to be turned on to share files and folders.

Turn on media sharing

Media are photos, music and videos, among other things. Media Sharing must be turned on to share media with others on your network.

1 Open the Network and Sharing Center.

2 Click the down arrow by Media sharing.

3 Click Change.

Media sharing   ○ Off

> When media sharing is on, people and devices on the network can access shared music, pictures, and videos on this computer, and this computer can find those types of shared files on the network.

Change... **3**

4 Click Share my media.

5 Click OK.

6 Set the sharing options and click OK.

? DID YOU KNOW?
You can share media only if your network is a 'private' network.

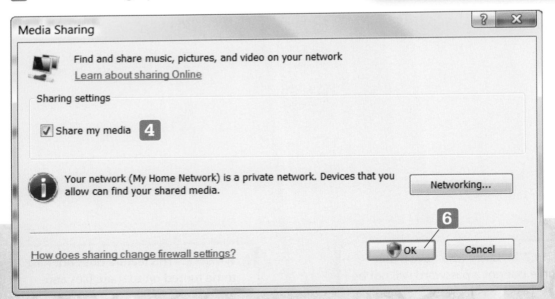

Media Sharing

Find and share music, pictures, and video on your network
Learn about sharing Online

Sharing settings

☑ Share my media **4**

Your network (My Home Network) is a private network. Devices that you allow can find your shared media.

Networking...

6

How does sharing change firewall settings?

OK   Cancel

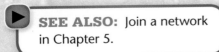

► SEE ALSO: Join a network in Chapter 5.

Save data to the Public folder

If you've enabled Public folder sharing, you'll want to save data to share in the Public folders.

1 Open a picture, document or other item you wish to save to the Public folders.

2 Click File and click Save As.

3 In the Save As dialogue box, click Public.

4 Select the Public subfolder to save to.

5 Type a name for the file.

6 Click Save.

 ALERT: In Windows Photo Gallery, you'll click File and Make a Copy.

HOT TIP: Save pictures to the Public Pictures folder. Save documents to the Public Documents folder.

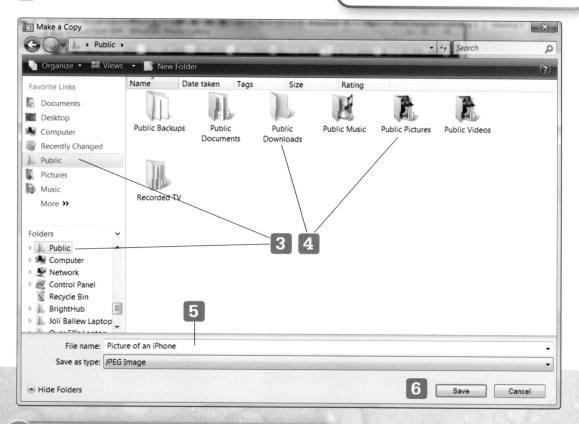

? DID YOU KNOW?

It's actually better to move data you want to share into the Public folders. That way, you won't create duplicate copies of the data on your hard drive.

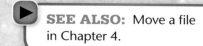
SEE ALSO: Move a file in Chapter 4.

Access the Public folder

You can access the Public folder by browsing to it. This may require you to browse the network if the Public folders are stored on another PC.

1 Click Start and click your user name.

2 Use the scroll bars in the left pane to locate Public.

3 Click Public.

4 Double-click the Public folder to open it.

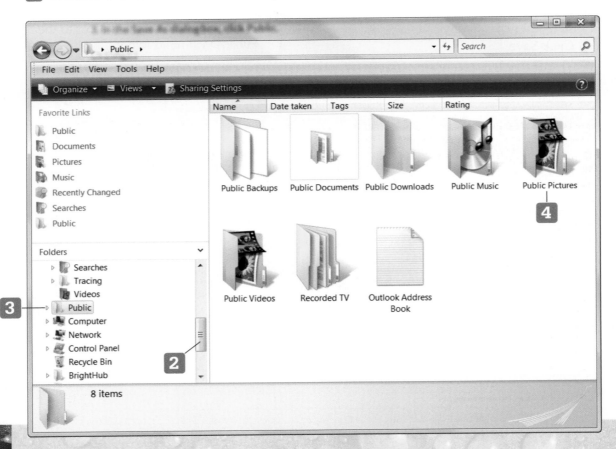

14 Fix problems

Enable System Restore

System Restore, if enabled, regularly creates and saves *restore points* that contain information about your computer that Windows uses to work properly. If your computer starts acting strangely, you can use System Restore to restore your computer to a time when it was working properly.

1 Click Start.

2 In the Start Search box, type System Restore.

3 Click System Restore under the Programs results.

4 Click open System Protection.

ALERT: System Restore can't be enabled unless the computer has at least 300 MB of free space on the hard disk, or if the disk is smaller than 1 GB.

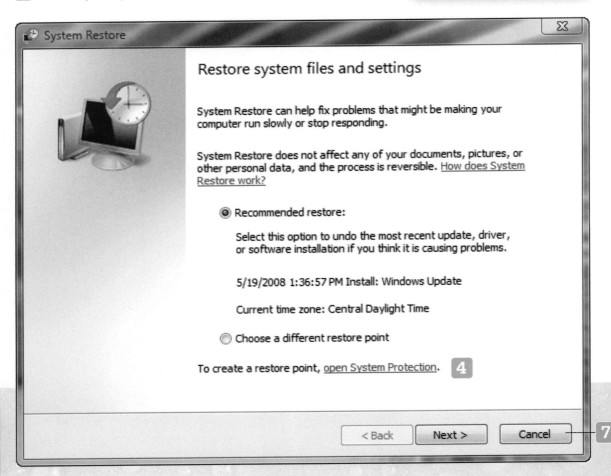

System Restore

Restore system files and settings

System Restore can help fix problems that might be making your computer run slowly or stop responding.

System Restore does not affect any of your documents, pictures, or other personal data, and the process is reversible. How does System Restore work?

◉ Recommended restore:

Select this option to undo the most recent update, driver, or software installation if you think it is causing problems.

5/19/2008 1:36:57 PM Install: Windows Update

Current time zone: Central Daylight Time

◯ Choose a different restore point

To create a restore point, open System Protection. **4**

< Back   Next >   Cancel   **7**

5 Verify that the C: drive, or the System drive, is selected. If it is not, select it.

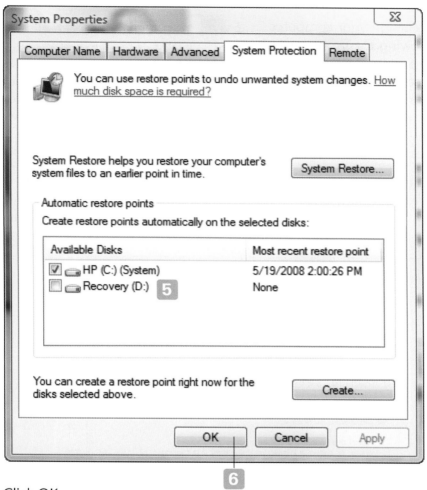

6 Click OK.

7 In the System Restore window, click Cancel.

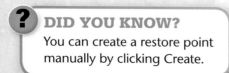

DID YOU KNOW?
You can create a restore point manually by clicking Create.

! ALERT: Create a restore point manually any time you think you're about to do something that may cause the computer harm, such as downloading and installing a third-party application.

Use System Restore

When a problem occurs on your computer your first step to resolving the problem is often System Restore. Use System Restore when you download and/or install software or hardware that causes a problem for the PC, or any time the computer seems unstable.

1 Open System Restore.

2 Click Next to accept and apply the recommended restore point.

3 Click Finish.

? DID YOU KNOW?
Because System Restore works only with its own system files, running System Restore will not affect any of your personal data. Your pictures, email, documents, music, etc. will not be deleted or changed.

? DID YOU KNOW?
System Restore is a 'system utility'. It cannot recover a lost personal file, email or picture.

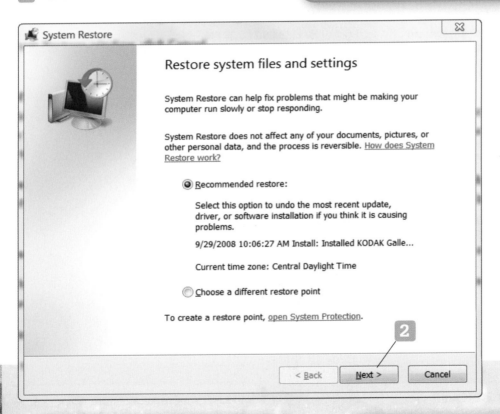

System Restore

Restore system files and settings

System Restore can help fix problems that might be making your computer run slowly or stop responding.

System Restore does not affect any of your documents, pictures, or other personal data, and the process is reversible. How does System Restore work?

◉ Recommended restore:

Select this option to undo the most recent update, driver, or software installation if you think it is causing problems.

9/29/2008 10:06:27 AM Install: Installed KODAK Galle...

Current time zone: Central Daylight Time

○ Choose a different restore point

To create a restore point, open System Protection.

2

< Back | Next > | Cancel

! ALERT: If you have a virus, System Restore probably won't work to resolve the problem, as viruses often attack personal files as well as system files.

! ALERT: If you are running System Restore on a laptop, make sure it's plugged in. System Restore should never be interrupted.

Disable unwanted start-up items

Lots of programs and applications start when you boot your computer. This causes the start-up process to take longer than it should, and programs that start also run in the background, slowing down computer performance. You should disable unwanted start-up items to improve all-around performance.

DID YOU KNOW?
Even if you disable a program from starting when Windows does, you can start it when you need it by clicking it in the Start and All Programs menu.

1 Click Start.

2 In the Start Search window, type System Configuration.

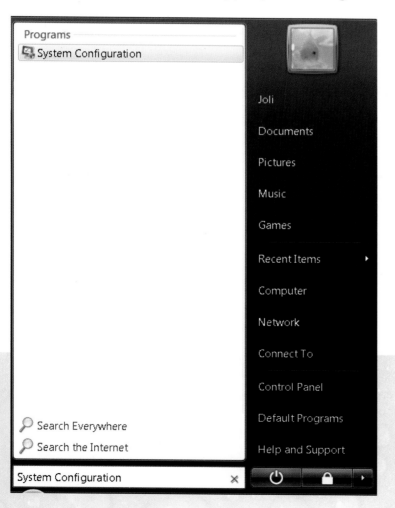

3 Under Programs, click System Configuration.

4 From the Startup tab, deselect third-party programs you recognise but do not use daily.

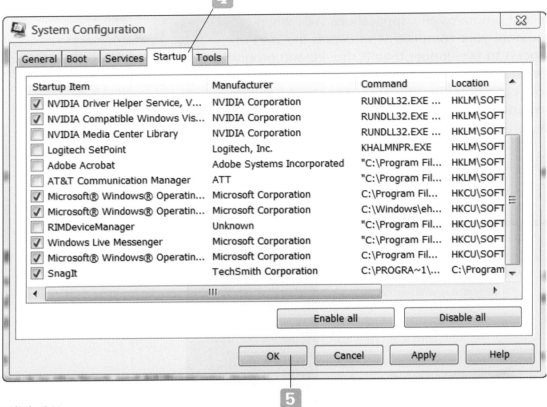

5 Click OK.

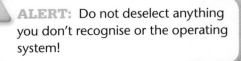

ALERT: Do not deselect anything you don't recognise or the operating system!

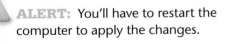

ALERT: You'll have to restart the computer to apply the changes.

Resolve Internet connectivity problems

When you have a problem connecting to your local network or to the Internet, you can often resolve the problem in the Network and Sharing Center.

1 Open the Network and Sharing Center.

2 Click the red X.

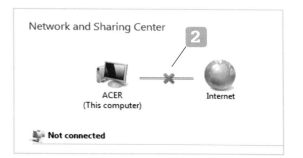

3 Perform the steps in the order they are presented.

> **ALERT:** Make sure your cable modem, router, cables and other hardware are properly connected, plugged in and turned on.

 SEE ALSO: Enable Network Discovery in Chapter 5.

> **ALERT:** You won't see a red X if the network is functioning properly.

 DID YOU KNOW?
Almost all the time, performing the first step will resolve your network problem.

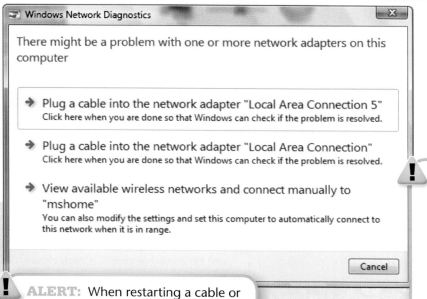

> **ALERT:** If prompted to 'reset' your broadband or satellite connection, turn off all hardware including the PC and restart them in the following order: cable/satellite/DSL modem, router, PCs.

> **ALERT:** When restarting a cable or satellite modem, remove any batteries to completely turn off the modem.

Use Device Driver Rollback

If you download and install a new driver for a piece of hardware and it doesn't work properly, you can use Device Driver Rollback to return to the previously installed driver.

1 Click Start.

2 Right-click Computer.

3 Click Properties.

ALERT: You can only rollback to the previous driver. This means that if you install a driver (D1) and it doesn't work and then you install another driver (D2) and it doesn't work, using Device Driver Rollback will revert to D1, not the driver before it.

SEE ALSO: Download and install a driver in Chapter 8.

ALERT: The Rollback driver option will be available only if a new driver has recently been installed.

4 Under Tasks, click Device Manager (not shown).

5 Click the + sign next to the hardware that uses the driver to rollback.

6 Double-click the device name.

7 Click the Driver tab.

8 Click Roll-Back Driver.

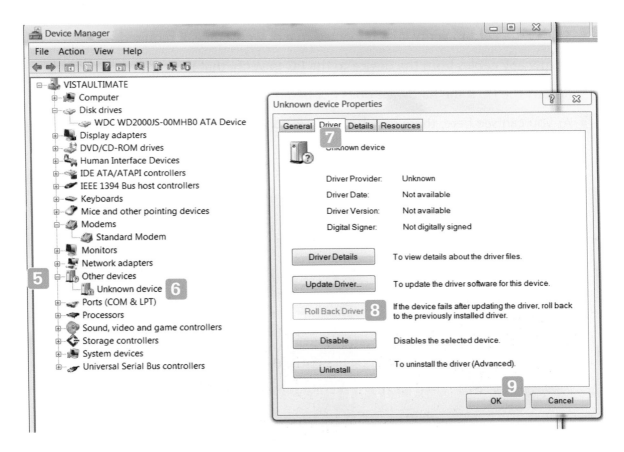

9 Click OK.

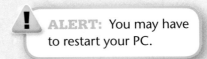

ALERT: You may have to restart your PC.

Reconnect loose cables

Many problems occur due to loose or disconnected cables. A mouse can't work unless it's plugged in or its wireless component is. A cable modem can't work unless it is connected securely to the PC and the wall. When troubleshooting, always check your connections.

1 Locate the hardware device that is not working.

2 Follow the cord to verify it is connected to a power source, if required.

3 Follow any cables from the device to the PC to verify that it is connected securely.

4 Restart the PC if the hardware does not begin to work within a few seconds.

5 As you can see here, there may be multiple connectivity points. You may find USB, FireWire, S-Video, and more.

! ALERT: If you aren't sure whether a cable is properly inserted, remove it and reinsert.

? DID YOU KNOW?
Many hardware items have multiple connections and connection types. If one type of connection doesn't work, like USB, try FireWire.

View available hard drive space

Problems can occur when hard drive space gets too low. This can become a problem when you use a PC to record television shows or movies (these require a lot of hard drive space) or if your hard drive is partitioned.

ALERT: If you find you are low on disk space, you'll have to delete unnecessary files and/or applications.

1 Click Start.

2 Click Computer.

3 In the Computer window, click the C: drive.

4 View the available space.

ALERT: If the drive is more than 85% full, delete or move some of the data on it, if possible.

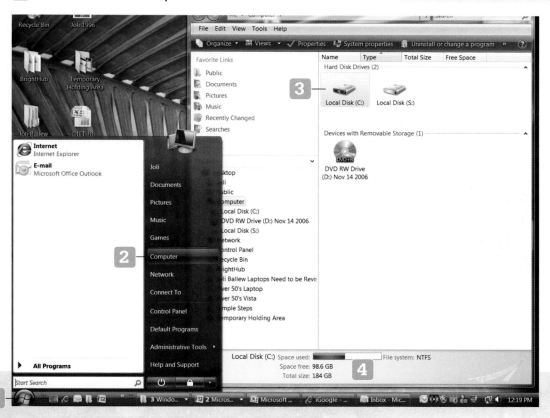

HOT TIP: If you see a second drive, as shown here, click it too; you may find you can move data from the C: drive to this one to recover much-needed space on the C: drive.

SEE ALSO: Move a file, Delete a file, Move a folder, Delete a folder, all in Chapter 4.

Uninstall unwanted programs

If you haven't used an application in more than a year, you probably never will. You can uninstall unwanted programs from Control Panel.

1 Click Start, click Control Panel.

2 In Control Panel, click Uninstall or change a program.

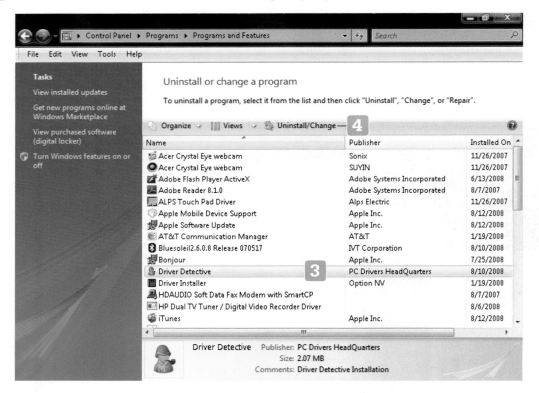

3 Scroll through the list. Click a program name if you want to uninstall it.

4 Click Uninstall/Change.

5 Follow the prompts to uninstall the program.

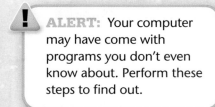 **ALERT:** Your computer may have come with programs you don't even know about. Perform these steps to find out.

 HOT TIP: Look for programmes in the list that start with the name of the manufacturer of your computer (Acer, Hewlett-Packard, Dell, etc.). You'll probably find programmes that the manufacturer installed. Some you may want to keep, but it's best to uninstall what you don't need.

Top 10 Vista Problems Solved

Problem 1: I saved a file and now I can't find it. I don't remember where it's saved

You need to perform a more advanced search:

1 Click Start.

2 In the Start Search window, type the name of the file.

3 If the file appears in the Start menu, click it once to open it.

4 If the files does not appear in the Start menu, click Search Everywhere.

5 Click the icon for the type of file you're looking for to narrow down the results.

6 Refine the search as necessary by typing in a new name for the file. Note that you can also type in a word inside the file.

Problem 2: I'm physically connected to a network or I am within range of a wireless one but I cannot access the network

You need to turn on Network Discovery.

1 Click Start.

2 In the Start Search window, type Network and Sharing Center. Note that what you type in the Start Search window does not need to be capitalised.

3 Under Sharing and Discovery, click the down arrow next to Off, by Network discovery. It will become an upwards arrow.

4 Click Turn on network discovery unless it is already turned on.

5 Click Apply.

6 Click the X to close the Network and Sharing Center.

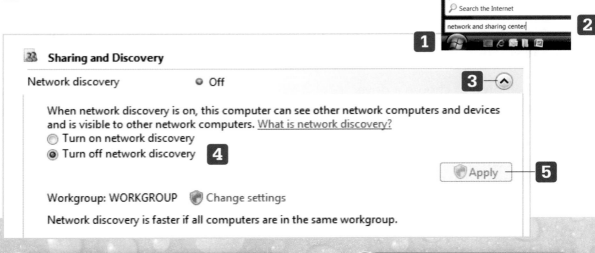

Programs
Network and Sharing Center

Search Everywhere
Search the Internet

network and sharing center **2**

1

Sharing and Discovery

Network discovery   Off   **3**

When network discovery is on, this computer can see other network computers and devices and is visible to other network computers. What is network discovery?
  Turn on network discovery
  Turn off network discovery **4**

Apply **5**

Workgroup: WORKGROUP   Change settings

Network discovery is faster if all computers are in the same workgroup.

? DID YOU KNOW?
The Network and Sharing Center is also where you set up file sharing, public folder sharing, printer sharing, password-protected sharing and media sharing.

? DID YOU KNOW?
You can click in the Tasks pane to view computers and devices on your home network and manage network connections.

Problem 3: My computer is running slower than normal

You need to run Disk Cleanup:

1 Click Start.

2 In the Start Search dialogue box, type Disk Cleanup.

3 In the results, under Programs, click Disk Cleanup.

4 Choose My files only to clean your files and nothing else. Choose Files from all users on this computer if you wish to clean additional users' files.

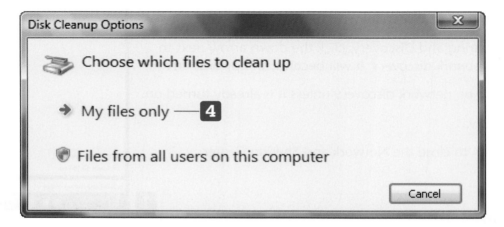

5 If prompted to choose a drive or partition, choose the letter of the drive that contains the operating system, which is almost always C: but occasionally D:. Click OK.

> **!** **ALERT:** You may not be prompted to choose a drive letter if only one drive exists.

6 Select the files to delete. Accept the defaults if you aren't sure.

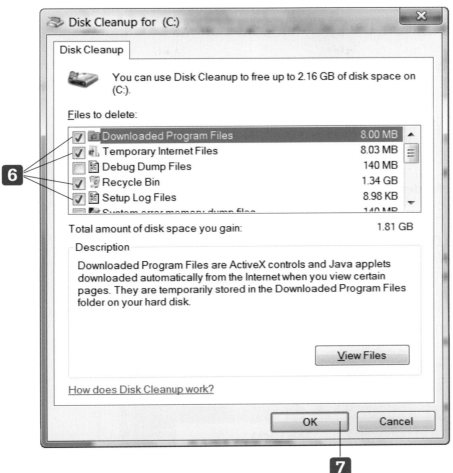

7 Click OK to start the cleaning process.

Problem 4: I think I might have a virus. How do I find out?

Scan for viruses with Windows Defender.

1 Click Start.

2 Click Control Panel.

3 Click Security.

4 Click Windows Defender.

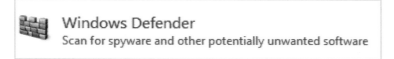

5 Click the arrow next to Scan (not the Scan icon). Click Full Scan if you think the computer has been infected.

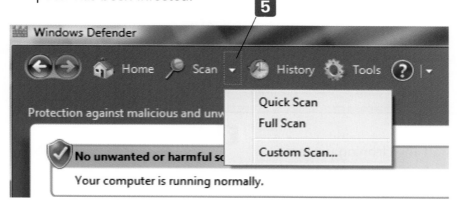

6 Click the X in the top right corner to close the Windows Defender window.

Problem 5: I want to watch TV on my computer but I can't. Why not?

You may not have a TV tuner installed and/or it may not be set up properly.

1. Click Start and click All Programs.

2. Click Media Center.

3. If you have not set up Media Center, work through the prompts.

4. If you have the proper hardware, the set-up process will prompt you to set up your TV tuner.

5. Complete the set-up process.

6. In the Media Center window, move to the right of recorded TV once and click live tv. If you receive an error when you click live tv, its either because you do not have the television signal properly set up or you don't have a TV tuner.

Problem 6: When I insert a CD, DVD or other media, I am either not prompted regarding what I'd like to do or I don't like the program or window that opens when the media is inserted

You need to change AutoPlay settings.

1 Click Start.

2 Click Default Programs. (It's on the Start menu.)

3 Click Change AutoPlay settings.

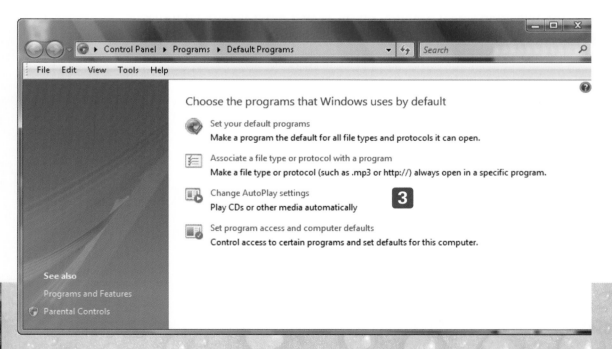

4 Use the drop-down lists to select the program to use for the media you want to play.

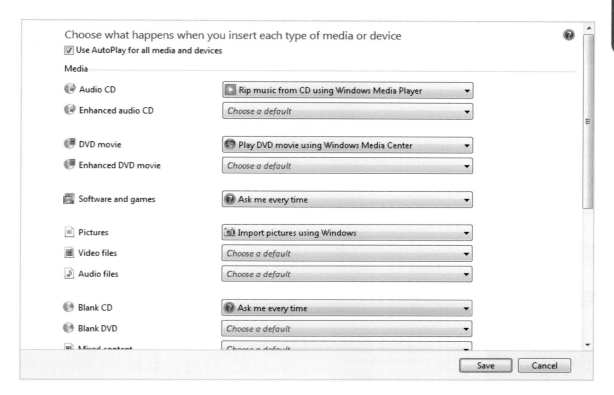

Choose what happens when you insert each type of media or device

☑ Use AutoPlay for all media and devices

Media

🔘 Audio CD	▶ Rip music from CD using Windows Media Player ▾
🔘 Enhanced audio CD	*Choose a default* ▾
📀 DVD movie	🔘 Play DVD movie using Windows Media Center ▾
📀 Enhanced DVD movie	*Choose a default* ▾
🗔 Software and games	❓ Ask me every time ▾
🖼 Pictures	📷 Import pictures using Windows ▾
🎞 Video files	*Choose a default* ▾
🎵 Audio files	*Choose a default* ▾
🔘 Blank CD	❓ Ask me every time ▾
🔘 Blank DVD	*Choose a default* ▾
🔘 Mixed content	*Choose a default* ▾

Save   Cancel

5 Click Save.

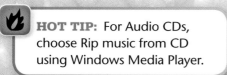

HOT TIP: For Audio CDs, choose Rip music from CD using Windows Media Player.

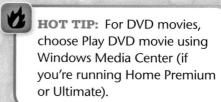

HOT TIP: For DVD movies, choose Play DVD movie using Windows Media Center (if you're running Home Premium or Ultimate).

Problem 7: I can't see, hear or navigate the computer the way I'd like to due to a disability

You can get recommendations to make the computer easier to use.

1 Click Start and in the Start Search window, type Ease.

2 Under Programs, click Ease of Access Center.

3 Click Get recommendations to make your computer easier to use.

4 Answer the questions as they are asked, clicking Next to move to the next screen.

5 Configure the recommended settings in the Ease of Access Center.

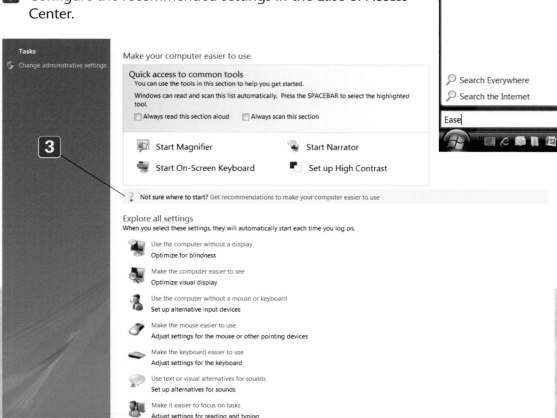

Problem 8: I have shared a printer but it still can't be accessed by other computers on my network

You need to enable printer sharing.

1 Open the Network and Sharing Center.

2 Click the down arrow by Printer sharing (it will change to an up arrow).

3 Click Turn on printer sharing.

4 Click Apply.

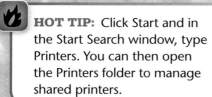

HOT TIP: Click Start and in the Start Search window, type Printers. You can then open the Printers folder to manage shared printers.

Problem 9: My computer is acting up. It was fine yesterday, but today I can't open my favourite program or access the Internet, or I have another problem

You need to run System Restore.

1 Open System Restore.

2 Click Next to accept and apply the recommended restore point.

3 Click Finish.

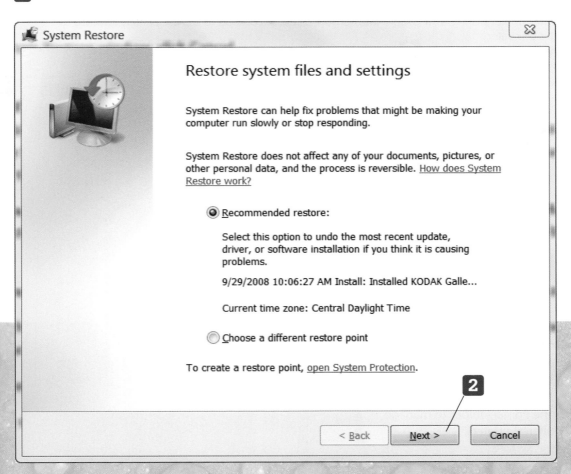

Problem 10: I can't connect to the Internet

You can troubleshoot Internet connectivity in the Network and Sharing Center.

1 Open the Network and Sharing Center.

2 Click the red X.

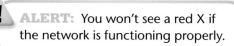

ALERT: You won't see a red X if the network is functioning properly.

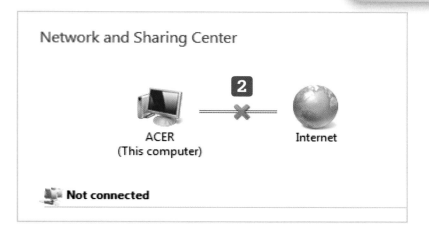

Network and Sharing Center

ACER
(This computer)

Internet

Not connected

3 Perform the steps in the order they are presented.

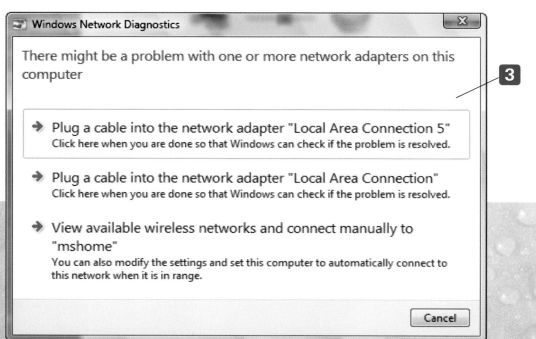

Windows Network Diagnostics

There might be a problem with one or more network adapters on this computer

3

➜ Plug a cable into the network adapter "Local Area Connection 5"
Click here when you are done so that Windows can check if the problem is resolved.

➜ Plug a cable into the network adapter "Local Area Connection"
Click here when you are done so that Windows can check if the problem is resolved.

➜ View available wireless networks and connect manually to "mshome"
You can also modify the settings and set this computer to automatically connect to this network when it is in range.

Cancel